24 June 2006,

To Barry,
Thank You for your
Service in Vietnam
with the 9th Inf Div.
With Deep Respect
In Brotherhood,
Ray Bows

# TIME-LINE VIETNAM

## VIETNAM

### The Tiger That Ate The Firebase

Master Sergeant Ray Bows, US Army, Retired

with

Pia Problemi

This book was written at the
Oceanside Inn, 8 Oceanside Drive, Scituate, Mass. 02066
www.BnBOceansideInn.Com
Our sincere thanks to Doris Crary and Dennis Badore
for their hospitality and kindness.
Dennis served in Vietnam in 1966-67 as a pole lineman
with the 1st Signal Brigade.

(See *The Pole-Cat and the Hawk MP* on page 121)

# TIME-LINE VIETNAM
## The Tiger That Ate The Firebase

Bows & Company Publishing, Ormond Beach, Florida

Preface by Brigadier General Joseph Stringham

ISBN 0-929973-03-8
Library of Congress Catalogue Card Number: TX 6-095-694
First Edition, July 2004

BOWS & COMPANY
P.O. Box 730183, Ormond Beach, Florida 32173-0183
Bowsandcompany@hotmail.com

This is a non-fiction work, however, some of the names of individuals have been changed and the dates of some events have been best guessed.

Tiger print by Specht, page viii. plate in possession of Bows & Company
Cover by Pia Problemi - photos of *Joel W. Mock, Robert J. Wiedemann &Ray Bows*

Previous Books by Ray Bows:

*US Allied Military Tokens of the Vietnam War, 1983*
*Vietnam Military Lore 1959-1973, Another Way To Remember, 1988*
*Vietnam Military Lore – In The Name of War, 1996*
*Vietnam Military Lore – Legends, Shadows and Heroes, 1997*

Printed in the United States of America

# Preface

For thousands of US service personnel, the American experience in Southeast Asia became a defining factor in our lives. In the fabric of the Cold War, the many nations involved in the defense of the Republic of Vietnam, witnessed their own embroilment in the issue of the war within their respective frontiers. In Southeast Asia the conflict caused the extermination of the Montagnard population and their culture, and the ruthless genocide of more than half the Cambodian people. Whatever the ills society may blame upon it, the war in Vietnam, marked the high water of Communism, and a victory for the policy of its containment. It was the definitive turning point in the Cold War in favor of the West.

Historical lessons in international politics, diplomacy and actual combat, provide glimpses of a major land war on the Asian subcontinent. The role American servicemen played was profound, resulting in a complete reshaping of the American military, and changing the manner in which the United States would fight future wars. The political futility of images of combat, intensified by derision at home, profoundly dictated and determined the transformations of entire societies.

In the popular portrayal of the war in Vietnam, and experiences in combat, there has been a proliferation of fiction and mythology, masquerading as historical fact, providing a morbid form of entertainment. Yet among the junk pop art and alleged factual portrayals of combat there are serious and thoughtful endeavors, which are both entertaining and honest.

In this regard, authors Ray Bows and Pia Problemi provide us with a sincere literary snapshot of the American GI in combat. Beyond Bows' first book on the American experience in Vietnam, *Vietnam Military Lore - Legends, Shadows and Heroes* these authors have taken yet another approach in the portrayal of reality. *Time-Line Vietnam - The Tiger That Ate The Firebase* is as riveting as its predecessor. As always, Ray Bows, has meticulously researched his work and it is absolutely accurate. This book is one veteran's story, poignant and mesmerizing, with a timelessness that will stir the memories of those who served and those who waited. For others, the flavor of the entire period is portrayed as potently as a spoonful of *nukmam*.

Ray Bows is a master story teller. *Time-Line Vietnam - The Tiger That Ate The Firebase* will leave you with some bittersweet memories, maybe even a lump in your throat, and a reminder of the GIs in one's life - living or dead - which you may have known.


Joseph Stringham
Brigadier General, US Army, Retired

Authors Note:

*Brigadier General Joe Stringham, known to his soldiers as "Smokin' Joe" served in Vietnam with Special Forces Detachment A-301, Ben Cat. A graduate of West Point, he spent many years with the US Army Rangers and Special Operations. In Vietnam, he formed a Chinese mercenary battalion, code name "MIKE FORCE," the first of its kind and the subject of the John Wayne movie,* The Green Berets. *General Stringham rose through the ranks to be assigned to foreign governments as a security representative for the Joint Chiefs of Staff. He holds two Distinguished Service Medals, and four Legions of Merit, seven combat decorations for valor including the Silver Star and six foreign decorations for meritorious service. He is mentioned in Hans Halberstadts' book* Green Berets at War, *Morley Safer's* Flashbacks *and is featured in Bows'* Vietnam Military Lore - Legends, Shadows and Heroes. *Several years ago he was inducted into the US Army Ranger Hall of Fame.*

# Prelude

Thirty years after returning from Vietnam, I encountered a Nam vet in a bar, who asked, "Did I tell you about the tiger that ate the firebase?" When I told him no, he said, "I'll tell you the story when I'm sober." Later, when I reminded him of it, he said, "I could never share that story. I must've been drunk." My solution to his tale too horrible to tell, was to invent my own metaphoric version which I wrote in verse. When we refrain from sharing details with those who know about certain circumstances, we leave the door open for others to draw their own conclusions.

Ray Bows

## THE TIGER THAT ATE THE FIREBASE

She was a yellow and black,
Carnivorous thriller,
A stealthy green-eyed,
Sleek, unfeeling killer,

This Tiger who gracefully
Padded through ponds,
Who daily ate frogs,
From perfect round fronds,

And, when on occasion,
They got woefully near,
She'd feast on her buffalo,
Her boar, and her deer.

She seemed so content,
In sun, wind and rain.
Empress of Forest,
And Queen of Domain,

But soldiers patrolled,
Into her jungle lair,
Her forest invaded,
How could they dare?

From a new base, artillery
dropped frequently near.
They picked up the pace,
They slaughtered her deer,

They destroyed all her forest,
With mortars and such,
Bombing and strafing –
It was all just too much.

Her hunting grounds gone,
And, her source of food,
The men changed the rules,
Dumb, cruel and crude.

Her boars were all dead,
Her buffalo gone,
She should have suspected
This all along.

With a dark but sharp gleam,
In her two piercing eyes,
Her feast at the base,
Would be their surprise!

The big cat approached them,
Their fate she would seal,
She would carry them off,
As her next gourmet meal.

She smelled strong aromas,
She could see when they'd fire,
She quietly crawled,
Right up to their wire.

She slipped passed their claymores,
And half sleeping guards,
She filled up her belly,
With men playing cards.

They all lost their minds,
As she bit off their heads,
She wasn't quite done,
More men slept in beds.

She ate them and chewed them
And tore flesh off their bones,
Until one man, her dessert,
Woke up all alone.

The Tiger had saved,
The best one for last,
The young man was fearful,
His cot he un-assed.

But the Tiger ensnared him,
And ate that young man,
Having eaten so much,
She left the boy's hand.

They sent reinforcements,
After her silent attack,
But the Tiger just left,
She never looked back.

They dropped in their mortars,
Their chain-mail and mace
To do away with the Tiger,
That terrorized that damned place.

The Army bureaucracy,
In this whole Tiger mess,
Thought the story back home,
Folks just could not digest.

"Your son died so cleanly,
So quiet, so quick,
I hope Mrs. Smithgerwatz,
This won't make you sick."

"A big Tiger ate him!
He smelled the beast's breath,
He fought and he screamed,
He screamed till his death."

"I hope Mrs. Smithgerwatz,
That we've made it quite clear,
A Vietnamese Tiger,
Ate your little dear."

Their pencils were sharpened,
Their erasers erased,
They'd never tell stories,
That would bring any disgrace.

"Your son's base was hit,
Mortars dropped in the sand,
We'll box up his belongings,
And most of his hand."

No, not one single Tiger,
Ate one single man,
Not in I Corps, or IV Corps,
Not in that whole land.

But, off the record,
There was just one case,
When one vengeful Tiger,
Ate one firebase.


This poem is dedicated to our beloved friend,
Jack Reed of Cleveland, Ohio who passed away 17 May 2003.

"I Have Seen War...I have seen blood running from the wounded...I have seen the dead in the mud. I have seen cities destroyed...I have seen children starving. I have seen the agony of mothers and wives. I Hate War."

From an inscription on the
Franklin Delanor Roosevelt Memorial,
Washington D.C.

# Dedicated to

## SP5 Robert J. Wiedemann, US Army
## and his family –
## Chester, Lillian, Bill, Marilyn, Betsy and Joe,

## and to

## PFC Joel W. Mock, USMC
## and his mother, Gertrude Mock Miller,

and the 1,523 sons of Indiana who died in Vietnam,
ninety-one of whom, like Bobby and Joel, were from Gary,
and to all those who served as military funeral escorts
during the Vietnam War.

\* \* \* \* \* \* \*

## Specialist Fifth Class Robert Joseph Wiedemann,
191st Military Intelligence Detach, 1st Cavalry Division, US Army,
was born 19 June 1948.
He was killed in action, north of Hué, Vietnam 25 March 1968.
His name is inscribed on the Vietnam Veterans Memorial
in Washington D.C. on the east wall, panel 46E, line 25.

\* \* \* \* \* \* \*

## Private First Class Joel W. Mock,
9th Motor Transport Battalion, 3d Marine Division, USMC,
was born 30 December 1946.
He was killed in action at Gio Linh, Vietnam 21 March 1967.
His name is inscribed on the Vietnam Veterans Memorial
in Washington D.C. on the east wall, panel 17E, line 9.

# Contents

*Photograph section follows page 86*

# Foreword

Throughout our lives we experience many diverse relationships with the people we encounter. If they end, we take with us the memories and the lessons learned from those experiences and move on. Why do some relationships fail? Perhaps, too often, we try to take control of the other person's life, hence, putting strain on the relationship. Isn't it far better to accept the person for whom they are and not try to mould them into the person we want them to be?

Since meeting Ray Bows, our relationship has been based on this principle. By accepting and not trying to mould each other, our friendship has grown, and our understanding, support and respect for one another has strengthened. Living with a war veteran is not always a smooth process, although it is discerning.

Having read many books about Vietnam veterans' experiences, and having watched real live footage of the circumstances thrust upon you, it is apparent to me how young you all were.

While watching *Letters Home From Vietnam,* I noticed the look on those young faces - a look that Hollywood can never capture. I realized that nations send their youth to fight *a man's war*, and when those wars are over the general public forgets, getting on with their lives, expecting the servicemen and women to do the same. Unfortunately, traumatic experiences do not simply go away, even with time, and the best one can hope for is that individual veterans learn to deal with their past. In understanding the after affects of trauma, such as those caused by war, and post-traumatic stress disorder (PTSD), which bring on nightmares and flashbacks, I have learned that the heroes are not only those who die during war, but also the survivors who carry invisible scars.

Ray Bows joined the Army in January 1963 at the age of seventeen. In 1968, he had already fulfilled his military obligation with four years of overseas service when he volunteered to go to Vietnam. I often wondered what motivated him to do such a gallant thing. This book evolved from persistent thoughts, and the question I finally asked Ray, "Why did you volunteer for Vietnam?"

At fifty-seven years old, driving from Washington, D.C. to the Veterans Medical Center in Boston for heart surgery, Ray told me about the events that drove him to become an active participant in the Vietnam War. For countless times after that I queried Ray about his experiences as he entrusted me with his memories. I respect him for sharing this part of his world with me, and encouraged him to share his story with others. The result is *Time Line Vietnam - The Tiger That Ate The Firebase.*

This is one soldier's experience in and around the combat zone. It touched and inspired me, and gave me new insight into war and events of the 1960's. This account was told to me in Ray's own words.

Today, when confronted with statements such as "War is wrong," and "War is not the answer," I ask myself, *What is the answer?* Until we truly learn to live with one another in peace, accepting and not trying to mould others into our ideals, I sadly believe that war will continue to happen.

A piece of my heart will always be with soldiers fighting for freedom and the service volunteers who support them. They, and their families, are due our utmost respect.

Peace always,

Pia Problemi
6 March 2003
London, England

# VIETNAM

Dien Bien Phu

HANOI

Gulf of Tonkin

DMZ Dong Ha

Khe Sanh

Hué

Da Nang

LAOS

SOUTH CHINA SEA

Pleiku

Qui Nhon

CAMBODIA

Nha Trang

Cam Ranh Bay

Tay Ninh

Bien Hoa Long Binh

Cu Chi Thu Duc

Dian SAIGON

My Tho

Can Tho

# CU CHI BASE CAMP
## Home of the 25th Infantry Division

JUNGLE

JUNGLE

N

3/13th Arty.

Combat Leadership School

1/8th Arty.

1/5th Mech. Inf. Trans. area

2/34th

15.

11.

12.

HQs 25th

25th Admin.

2/27th Inf.

Ammo Point

25th Avn. POL.

CU CHI AIRFIELD

242d Avn. CH-47's

10.

25 MP

8.

25th Med. Bn.

12th Evac.

9.

725th Maint. Motor Pool

68th Engr.

14. CH-47's

6/77th Arty.

554th Engrs.

CH-47's

6.

7.

3/4th Cav.

13.

4.

25th S & T

5.

DISCOM

2.

1.

3.

TTP

To Hoc Mon, Dian and Long Binh

To Hobo Woods and Tay Ninh

16.

17.

1. Trailer Transfer Point
2. Division Support Command
3. Our position on perimeter night of 25 February 1969
4. Oncoming NVA forces night of 25 February 1969
5. Outside Movie Theatre
6. 25th S & T Battalion
7. 725th Maintenance Motor Pool
8. 25th Medical Battalion
9. Road where Navy chopper crashed
10. 25th Military Police Company –
    barracks were damaged by 20mm rockets
11. 2/34th Armored Battalion
12. 25th Division Headquarters
13. 554th Engineer Battalion
14. 242d Muleskinner Helicopter Pad
15. Abandoned bunker outside perimeter used by VC
16. Eastern end of the Village of Cu Chi
17. Area where bodies were dumped and eventually buried

# Introduction

My story about Vietnam is not just about "flash-backs," it is also about Vietnam "flash-forwards." My vivid memories of those times are arranged in random flashes, from the last days of March and the first days of April 1968, until my return from the combat zone in June 1969. My once closely guarded memories are arranged in the same chaos that I still·live them. They materialize in the manner a youngster locates scenes on a video recorder by fumbling with the buttons **Fast Forward ▸ ▸** and **◂ ◂ Rewind**, which never give exactly the same results twice. If I was to share the story of my most profound experiences, they had to be in the order that I remember them, which does not have much order at all. My mind flashes back, then, flashes forward to events relevant to earlier circumstances.

What motivated me to share all this in the year 2003? My experiences were drawn out of me by Miss Pia Problemi, who has become such an important person in my life, and who has a profound need to understand the Vietnam War for herself. Current world events may also have been a factor, and I recognize that the difference in the way our servicemen were seen during the Vietnam War and the way they are seen now is astonishing.

Because of all my suppressed memories, and because my interviews do not always follow a rigid chronological order, it was suggested that a time-line might be helpful to the reader. That Time-Line, which appears on page 132-133, made me realize that I need a road map to my inner thoughts almost as much as those privy to my story would.

I was reluctant to share the finite details of my experiences with my interviewer, then, while listening to the radio; I was inspired by the discernable lyrics from Aerosmith's song, *Just Push Play* - "Just push play - F'n A - They're gonna bleep it anyway!"

I am grateful to Pia for not bleeping my words, for her handling of the experiences that I entrusted her with, and I appreciate her diligent and descriptive work.

Ray Bows
13 August 2003
Ormond Beach, Florida

# TIME-LINE VIETNAM
## THE TIGER THAT ATE THE FIREBASE

▶ **Play - Bien Hoa, South Vietnam – 8 June 1968**

There was a knot in my stomach and an uneasy feeling of anticipation as the *Flying Tiger 707* touched down at Bien Hoa Air Base. The screech of the wheels brought to perspective the realization that my one-year tour of duty had begun. It was a welcome sound after a long flight from Travis Air Force Base, California, and the straight drop out of the sky to Bien Hoa. It seemed as if the pilot began the commercial aircraft's descent only when we were directly over the air base. Landings like this one were common practice because of snipers at the end of the runway.

The doors of the aircraft opened. The temperature immediately started to rise. I grabbed my gear and made my way to the door with three hundred other servicemen, some who had been here before. I remember walking through the door of the aircraft as being one of the most vivid experiences of my Vietnam tour. It was midday, and I had just walked into a giant oven, the pungent smell of fish and fertilized rice paddies; the hundred-degree-plus temperature and heavy humid air nearly took my breath away. As we stood on the tarmac waiting to board buses, I could feel my sweat and the dust that was everywhere combining to form a layer of grime accumulating on my skin. The buses looked like flat-nosed school buses, but were olive drab in color. They had wire and bars on the open windows to keep grenades from being thrown inside during our twenty-minute trip through Bien Hoa City to the 90th Replacement Battalion at Long Binh.

Bien Hoa City lay in ruin, a result of the 1968 Tet Offensive. Three months after the attacks, the Vietnamese were still cleaning up the rubble, while Vietnamese women with babies strapped to their backs, were foraging through burnt garbage for food. Soldiers on the buses were astonished seeing the remnants of buildings riddled with holes from rockets and automatic weapons fire. The area had the starkness of a moonscape. I could hear what the men around me were saying, but I didn't see the reactions on their faces because, I too, was staring at the buildings, and wondering how I would adjust to this alien place.

Within minutes, we arrived at the 90th Replacement Battalion, which sat on a knoll of red clay. The camp was devoid of most trees and plants. There were wood frame barracks, and other buildings, as well as bunkers. Mustering areas, where morning and afternoon formations were held, were nothing more than large dirt lots bearing signs with, then strange sounding names, *Da Nang – Can Tho – Nha Trang* and *Pleiku,* among them. Everywhere I looked there were bullhorns mounted on poles, which announced spur of the moment formations, troop movements and flight departure times.

There were three kinds of soldiers here: the cadre and staff, snapping around with purpose; the GI's arriving, still with bewilderment of innocence and apprehension on their faces; and the soldiers processing out to go home, most with leather-like skin and thousand yard stares. I could tell who was who at a glance – there was absolutely no question.

The night belonged to the Viet Cong and my first experience in the dark was spent in and out of a bunker at the 90th, with enemy fire being launched from around the compound – mortars and rockets mainly. We wouldn't be issued weapons until we arrived at our units, and I had no idea what my assignment would be. Mentioning President Lyndon B. Johnson's recent visit to Vietnam, I jokingly told my new acquaintance, Staff Sergeant Robinson,

"If Cam Ranh Bay is safe enough for L.B.J, then it'll be safe enough for me."

The next day, at afternoon formation, we moved one step closer to our final destination. I received orders for the 4th Transportation Command, Saigon Port, and it sounded as good as Cam Ranh Bay. Robinson got his marching papers as well. He was being sent north to Qui Nhon. Robinson and I had only met on the airplane on our way to Nam, but had become fast friends. Neither of us liked the idea of splitting up.

Late in the afternoon, we boarded a bus for the 537th Personnel Services Company at Camp Zinn. We were billeted in sixteen-man "GP-Medium" tents, which had huge holes dry-rotted out of their tops and sides. We sat on our sheetless, pillowless cots and reminisced about landing in Okinawa's Kadena Air Base. During refuel we hit the Kadena NCO Club, ordering steaks and beers for breakfast. Okinawa had been our last stop before Vietnam and we took it for as much as we could get.

We also spoke about the assassination of Senator Robert Kennedy. Two days earlier, we had witnessed the shooting live on television in one of the Oakland Army Terminal day rooms. That was on 5 June. A day later we heard the announcement of his death, just before we boarded buses headed for Travis Air Force Base and our flight to this fucking shit hole.

At 2330 hours it began raining and we turned our cots on their sides to keep them dry, but it didn't do any good. The rain poured into our tent. It lasted a half an hour and when I finally laid down, my clothing, my boots, and my cot were all soaked. I fumbled around trying to get comfortable and eventually dozed off to sleep.

Suddenly, there was total chaos. Sirens were going off, and I wasn't sure where I was. Finally, I got my bearings and rushed to a bunker. It had a spectacular view of the happenings on the perimeter. Viet Cong were trying to get through the maze of concertina wire and mines, and they had set off clay-mores in the process. Aerial flares, and green and orange tracers, converged on the perimeter's edge lighting the darkness. Because of all the rain prior to the attack, I was standing waist-deep in water, in a bunker half above and half below the ground. There were things in the bunker swimming around, but I couldn't tell what they were. *Rats? Snakes? Maybe leeches?* I thought to myself, *Only 363 days to go!*

Just then we heard shouting,

"You green troops get out of that bunker! Out of that defensive position! Now! Move it! Back up the hill! Go to the cement latrines on the other side of the road!"

Flares were still going off and we were lit up brighter than daytime. I realized I was barefoot. Because of the rainstorm and the gaping holes in our tent, everything had gotten soaked, and I had taken my combat boots and socks off. When the sirens went off, I hadn't heard them. Robinson had rousted me off my bunk, but I couldn't find my combat boots. Now, I was the only one running around without boots on.

"Over by the latrines...Over by the latrines," we heard the voice shout again.

I scrambled for the road that was elevated higher than the rest of the area. The latrines were on the other side. As I climbed up the roadbed, small sharp stones careened under my bare feet, cutting them. I grappled on all fours, trying to make it to the top. For every two feet advanced, I'd slide back one. My feet were cold, wet and cut.

Just before I got to the top of the road-surface a thought flashed through my mind,

*Don't make your silhouette visible on the skyline any longer than you have to. Your back's to the enemy. You don't have a weapon. You don't have your combat boots on. And in another instant you'll be silhouetted.*

I vaulted across the road, then leaped into the blackness on the other side. Although, I didn't know it at the time, the jump, like my year in Vietnam, was both the longest and shortest leap of my life. I couldn't see the ground and I had no idea how long the fall would be. For a split-second the drop seemed to go on forever. In the same way, I couldn't imagine ever returning to the states.  This next year would be an eternity. . .

Then I hit damned near face first, rolling in the dirt and rock.  I cut the palms of my hands and tore all ten nails off my toes.  I picked myself up from my fall and limped into the latrine.  My toes were bloody stumps.  They were still numb.  I could see I was dragging blood across the latrine floor.  I thought, *What am I doing here? – How the Hell did I get here?*

Between the aerial flares, which cast shapes and shadows across the compound on this moonless night, there were intervals of pitch black.  The Viet Cong (VC) and North Vietnamese Army (NVA), when setting up mortar or rocket positions, used this darkness as a weapon.

I ripped off pieces of my T-shirt and wrapped up my toes.    I realized how badly my face and hands hurt when Robinson asked me if I was OK.  Everything was beginning to throb now but I told him I was alright.  I tried to turn my mind to *Stateside* thoughts, but I wasn't having pleasant ones.

Soaked to the bone, in pain, and still bleeding, I had a flash of thought back to the orders assigning me to Vietnam.  At the age of twenty-two, my orders bore my name and service number, and read, in parentheses, "VOL."    I was a Vietnam "Volunteer!"  Did I really volunteer for this?  What motivated me to request Vietnam as an assignment?  I knew the answer then, and I know it now, but for thirty-five years I wasn't willing to share my story with anyone.  Now, in 2003,  the circumstances that pulled me into the slipstream that was Vietnam still punctuate my memories - memories of the most extended and yet most abbreviated year of my life.

By 3 a.m. the firing had tapered off. I looked out the door of the latrine. The night was calm, but still dark as black felt. I thought about the black felt armband and pallid-white gloves I had been issued when assigned to funeral escort detail. Two months earlier, I had escorted the body of a soldier killed in Vietnam home to his family. Only in Nam two days now, I was seriously wondering if I'd end up like that dead soldier.

The black armbands issued to military escorts were worn on uniforms at all times during funeral detail. The gloves were worn in public in the presence of the casket, specifically at the burial ceremony. Soldiers dreaded the duty of escorting bodies from Oakland, California to Hometown USA. Escort duty was mentally taxing, and could be one of the toughest jobs ever devised by the United States Army. During wartime, it was also one of the most necessary. Although the black armbands officially represented the black of grief and mourning, they also implied the foreboding and the unknown.

But, not least of all, the black armbands represented the black of a lie. During Vietnam, families would seldom be told the truth. The military would decide what was best for them. "Your son died instantly – he never suffered." Sons or husbands never screamed in pain; they never slowly bled to death on the battlefield; their bodies were never chopped to pieces by enemy fire; tigers never ate firebases. Each soldier died quickly, instantly, painlessly, and heroically. In the 1960s, it was the Army's way - The Army Standard.

Families didn't want the gory details, but they *did* want the truth, even though they seldom got it. The entire parody of military balderdash was a prelude to the Army, cutting all ties with families of fallen soldiers. After the last volley was fired in tribute; after Taps was played; and after the "Stars and Stripes" was presented, soldiers on funeral detail left the gravesite and families were left on their own. Never again would Uncle Sam feel a need to be in contact with them about their son's death. I know, because I was supposed to be a participant in one such severance. The problem was, I couldn't cut the connection.

### ◄◄ Rewind, Fort Leonard Wood, Missouri – March 1968

Two and a half months before my Vietnam tour began, I received instructions at Fort Leonard Wood from the Transportation Officer, Captain Kelly Cannon, to report to Headquarters Special Troops Orderly Room. I liked the captain, a bull of a man, who was firm, even-handed and intelligent.

While stationed in Europe, after my first duty assignment – Korea, I had impressed my bosses with my actions in troop movement. Seen as a soldier concerned about the needs of fellow soldiers, I was promoted ahead of my peers. At Gare de L'Est, the east train station in downtown Paris, France, my job was to get troops fed, billeted and shipped out in a timely manner, and I took my duties very seriously. At twenty-one, I made Staff Sergeant E-6 with only four years in the Army, before the days of production line "Shake & Bake NCOs." In January 1967, I was promoted along with veterans who had enlisted in the mid-1950s, some with up to eight years in grade.

Unknown to me, when I arrived at Fort Leonard Wood, it seemed to some that, as a twenty-two year old staff sergeant, I was out of character. I was seen more as a specialist four type. Captain Cannon liked me well enough, although, time-in-grade-wise, I outranked the then current NCOIC, Staff Sergeant Henley. Captain Cannon gave no indication that the position of NCOIC at post transportation was, by all rights, mine. Henley was ten years older than I was, but I didn't learn I outranked him until I received my orders for Vietnam. It was then that Captain Cannon came clean about denying me the position with his silence, as he wished me "Godspeed."

I'm certain Captain Cannon's actions resulted because I seemed too young to be the NCOIC. Certainly, it was in the best interest of the operation to retain Henley where he was. In Captain Cannon's eyes, Henley was more qualified for the position.

It appeared that Captain Cannon didn't know the reason that I had to report to the orderly room. If he did, he didn't let on. He just passed the word to me.

*Oh Shit,* I thought. *It's because I made a stink about attending the mandatory formation to march to the Bob Hope Show.* My reaction to that one was, *mandatory formation to see Bob Hope – Bullshit!*

As I understood it, back then, comedian Bob Hope had done a lot for the American figthing man, voluntarily entertaining troops in far flung corners of the world with his annual Christmas shows, but a mandatory formation to march to his performance stuck in my craw.

I stood by my principles, until the First Sergeant told me,

"You *will* muster in front of the orderly room with all the other NCOs, and you *will* march with the troops to the main parade field where the show is being held. However, you don't have to stay and see the show."

Yeah, like once there, I'd walk away. Well, I did! I knew there was something wrong with the rationale behind a mandatory formation to see Bob Hope. After marching the two miles, when we hit the main parade field, I broke ranks and just walked off, exactly like the first sergeant said I could. I didn't believe I was doing it, and he couldn't believe it either!

Even though I walked off the way I did, I was torn between doing the right thing and doing the wrong thing, between really wanting to see Bob Hope's performance and not wanting to be ordered to do something that should have been voluntary. I really believed there were certain things that the military shouldn't be able to make mandatory, and seeing the Bob Hope Show was one of them.

This incident at Fort Leonard Wood wouldn't be the first time or the last, that my superiors saw me as trouble. Now, my unwillingness to play the game had come back to haunt me. What other reason would they have for summoning me to the orderly room? Yet, I never saw the First Sergeant, or the CO, or anyone else in authority. I didn't get my ass chewed. This wasn't about being a team player! Or was it?

I was handed orders sending me on temporary duty (TDY). Assigned to funeral escort detail – I was ordered to report to

Oakland, California – pick up the remains of a dead soldier – and to return his remains to his family somewhere in the United States. I had never heard of such a thing, and as I walked out of the orderly room, I held the twenty or so copies of my orders in my right hand, as though reading them, as I stared into a blur of disbelief.

I don't remember getting my Class-A uniform squared away for my duties or spit shining my shoes, and spin shining my brass, but I know I did those things. I vaguely remember flying directly from Fort Leonard Wood, but no recollection, if I changed planes in St. Louis or Kansas City. No recall of the airport or the airline. I don't remember the ongoing flight to San Francisco, but I know all those things happened.

I do recall ensuring that the black felt armband was properly affixed to my uniform. I remember getting it tight up under my armpit. It had two snaps and was held in place with a large concealed safety pin. The armband had a fuzzy uncomfortable feeling about it. This whole thing had a bad feeling right from the start.

As I pinned the arm band in place, I wondered how my role as escort would play out. What was I supposed to do? When would I be briefed? What would be the extent of my involvement with the family of a deceased soldier I had never known? I wondered if I could carry out my duties in an acceptable way. It seemed that this was all about me, but it wasn't about me at all. It was about a family somewhere in the United States waiting for their loved-one's remains to come home.

**Flash-forward ► ►   Oakland, California - 31 March 1968**

My next recollection was being billeted at Oakland Army
Terminal.    There were hundreds of other soldiers, mostly
sergeants and some officers, pooled from army installations
across the United States to perform duties as military escorts.
Their purpose: sign for the body of a soldier and escort him
home.   The rank of the escort had to be equal or higher to that
of the deceased.

The mission of mortuary services, in the Republic of Vietnam,
began with the establishment of graves registration collection
points at Tan Son Nhut and Da Nang air bases. These collection
points received, processed, identified and evacuated deceased
US military servicemen, as authorized by the Commander, US
Military Assistance Command - Vietnam (MACV). From
January 1961 to July 1965, mortuary services in Vietnam were
provided by the US Air Force and accomplished by a civilian
mortician on temporary duty from Clark Air Base, Philippines,
who prepared bodies for stateside shipment in a small two-room
mortuary at Tan Son Nhut Air Base.

By 1963, the death rate of Americans in Vietnam had increased
to the extent that full time staffing of the mortuary was
necessary.   Staffing included one US Air Force civilian
mortician, one US Army graves registration NCO, and two
Vietnamese employees.

In 1965, the mortuary at Tan Son Nhut was expanded. The
Pentagon recognized that the responsibility for graves
registration should be transferred from the Air Force to the
Army, reasoning that the preponderance of deaths among US

forces in Vietnam were Army loses.  By 1 July 1966, transfer of the operation from the Air Force to the Army was completed. In Vietnam, mortuary facilities were established at Camp Redball, north of Tan Son Nhut, and on 20 June 1967, a second mortuary was opened at Da Nang Air Base.

Bodies of servicemen were flown from Vietnam, in a timely manner, to Travis Air Force Base, California.  Deceased US Army soldiers were then transferred to Oakland Army Terminal.  Processing at Oakland included cosmetizing, dressing and casketing dead soldiers.  Remains were then assigned a military escort who traveled with the casket to the place of final disposition as designated by the appropriate family representative.  This process from battlefield to hometown funeral home required seven to ten days.

The quarters at Oakland hadn't changed much since I had been there five years earlier on my way to Korea.  The paint on the walls had changed from light grey to light yellow or maybe light yellow to light blue, but the billets certainly seemed  more depressing this time.  I could look out the large windows across the hard-stand where formations were held and to the warehouse where the bodies of soldiers were stored.  I had looked forward to going to Korea in July 1963, but I wasn't looking forward to this duty at all.

We were issued an "Escort Duty Handbook," or instruction Sheet, or whatever.  I don't really remember what it looked like.  It's not something you save as a memento of your military career.  I do remember the instructions in it – printed to accompany the briefings we attended.

"I was seen, by my superiors, as a soldier concerned about the welfare of other soldiers and promoted ahead of my contemporaries." 30 January 1967, Camp Des Lodges, France - Ray Bows, is promoted to staff sergeant, as he peers between fellow soldiers, while Lieutenant Colonel Leslie Enoch, Commander, US Army Post Paris, congratulates the new E-6s.

## *Escort Duty Instructions*

1.  *The potential of having one of two types of coffins exists: The standard military aluminum coffin or the "soft-pack," a canvas bag used when bodies are flown to funeral homes in remote areas on small single engine aircraft – the actual coffin will be furnished by the funeral home upon arrival.*

2.  *If the escort is assigned a closed casket, he is to advise the family that every effort has been made to identify their loved-one. The Department of the Army strongly recommends that the seal on the coffin not be disturbed and the coffin not be opened. The escort is to stress that every possible means has been made to identify the service member and that nothing can be accomplished by breaking the casket's seal. However, the final decision to break the seal and view the body ultimately lies with the next of kin.*

3.  *The escort will precede the deceased, walking four steps in front of the casket, during ceremonies, each and every time the casket moves.*

4.  *A Survival Assistance Officer (SAO), an honor guard, a rifle team, and a bugler will be provided by the appropriate military service, generally the closest military installation to the family home.*

5.  *The US Government will provide the headstone marker, and United States flag.*

In the Army, it's pretty much a given that you take the good with the bad. You do what you're told and hope for the best, but you're always ready for the worst. Sometimes the light at the end of the tunnel is the headlight of an oncoming train. I was beginning to feel like a *man on a pitch fork*.

"Daddy, play *Man on a Pitch Fork* with us," my sons, Scott and Jeff would ask me when they were really little. "Okay, but remember kids, when you hear something good shout 'Yeeeaaa!' and when you hear something bad shout 'Boooo!'"

*A man was flying in an airplane high in the air...*
*YEEEAAA...!*
*But, the airplane ran out of fuel...*
*BOOOOO...!*
*But, the man managed to jump out...*
*YEEEAAA...!*
*But, he didn't have a parachute...*
*BOOOOO...!*
*As he fell to earth, he was headed directly for a haystack...*
*YEEEAAA...!*
*But, there was a pitchfork in the haystack...*
*BOOOOO...!*
*But, he missed the pitchfork...*
*YEEEAAA...!*
*But, he missed the haystack...*
*BOOOOO!*

"Staff Sergeant Ray A. Bows is to escort the body of SP5 Robert J. Wiedemann, killed in action in the Republic of South Vietnam, 25 March 1968. Staff Sergeant Bows will proceed via air from San Francisco International Airport to O'Hare International Airport, Chicago, Illinois, and continue to

Gary, Indiana via ground transportation provided by the funeral home."

When I was assigned as escort to a soldier I knew only as a name, it was like *Man on a Pitch Fork,* the game I used to play with my sons. I didn't know whether to applaud or object – to cheer or "boo!" I didn't know how his body would be packed and I had no idea if I drew a white soldier, an Hispanic, a Native American or an Afro-American. The year 1968 was charged with racial tensions. Escort duty had the potential to put soldiers in the middle of ethnic confrontations and some of the most notorious inner-city ghettos in America.

> *I finally knew where I was going...*
> *YEEEAAA...!*
> *But, I might get a "soft-pack"...*
> *BOOOOO...!*
> *But, I didn't...*
> *YEEEAAA...!*
> *But, Gary, Indiana was the inner city...*
> *BOOOOO...!*
> *"Wiedemann" sounded like an Anglo-Saxon name...*
> *YEEEAAA...!*
> *But, maybe I'd have to deal with a family and funeral*
> *that had customs unfamiliar to me...*
> *BOOOOO...!*
> *Then, I learned that Bobby Wiedemann was Caucasian...*
> *YEEEAAA...!*
> *But, then I learned that he was in a closed casket*
> *BOOOOO!*

Another day went by before I knew if I missed the pitchfork or not.

One of the most important aspects of casualty reporting in Vietnam was the accurate identification of the remains of deceased soldiers. Any improper identification resulted in added grief to the next of kin and caused "unnecessary embarrassment to the military." The wearing of dog tags and properly marked boots and clothing in Vietnam, and the carrying of identification cards were important in identifying remains.

Although, command emphasis was placed on these requirements, by the time instructions reached soldiers in the field, they lost their momentum and meaning, and were generally ignored by the troops. No one wanted to think of themselves as the next member of their squad who'd go home in a box. Even in basic training, soldiers had no idea of the reason they had to mark their boots and belts. They were never told that it was to identify their bodies if they were killed in combat. Military surveys disclosed that less than fifty per cent of military human remains, during the Vietnam War, had dog tags and ID cards when recovered, and that less than ten per cent had identifying marks on their boots and belts.

An important means of identification was fingerprinting. The proven reliability of fingerprints made them an invaluable tool in the mortuary's identification process. During 1968, seventy per cent of the cases processed (5,033 of 7,241) at the Tan Son Nhut mortuary, were identified by fingerprints. Other important means of identifying remains against official dental records and dental charts was a tedious and time consuming process, but one of the most effective.

The absence of a soft-pack was a plus and no matter what your ethnicity, getting a family of your same race was another big plus. A closed casket was definitely a minus. Escort duty, the toughest military duty I ever performed, would ultimately be determined by three factors – (1) the family's attitude toward their son's military service, (2) their attitude towards the Army, and (3) their attitude towards the escort who brought their loved one home.

At Oakland, stories of closed casket funerals were current scuttlebutt. Rumor had it, that bodies had been mixed up and a black Chicago family had buried a white soldier. The family had taken the Army at its word, not opened the coffin, and believed they were burying their son. It wasn't until a Caucasian family insisted on opening their son's coffin and discovered an Afro-American soldier inside, that the switch was reported in the newspapers.

Another account circulating at Oakland supposedly happened in Detroit. A soldier's brother was so distraught, that he began firing a pistol at those in uniform in attendance at the funeral. He wounded the military escort and killed several family members, including one woman who was his, and, of course, the dead soldier's mother.

In March 2003, I talked to the former NCOIC of the Detroit Army Funeral Operation, which handled all funerals in the greater Detroit area in 1967 and 1968. He did not remember any such incident happening, not in Detroit, but I do distinctly remember the story circulating at Oakland.

In March 1968, stateside racial tensions and military escort duty walked hand in hand. The major topic of conversation among both Afro-American and Caucasian escorts was that the US

Army was doing its best to defuse racial problems by assigning blacks to blacks and whites to whites, and we wanted to believe it, regardless of the rumors.

During our break in the indoctrination, we walked over to the mess hall to get something to eat. A group of us sat at a table, as one older NCO, a guy that everybody seemed to be avoiding, joined us. Generally, I always had something to say, but not today. I was too intent on listening. I hadn't figured all this out yet, and I wanted to learn all I could. When the conversation got round to the older NCO, I was surprised to learn that he had voluntarily been escorting bodies for over a year.

"Just another job," he said, "temporary duty money is good. I just stay in the background until the funeral is over. I enjoy the travel and Uncle Sam owes me lots of back TDY pay. I've got vouchers on my last three trips still to submit...and, you know, you always pad things a little...and, you know what? I don't care what race they are."

I couldn't believe it, but I kept my mouth shut. This callous bastard took the whole thing so impersonally. How could a soldier use the deaths of other soldiers to rack up big bucks in TDY pay? It was bad enough if you drew this as a one-time detail, but how could anyone volunteer and make a living doing it? I couldn't eat my lunch. Totally disgusted, I just wanted to go outside to get some fresh air, but, just then, a Special Forces sergeant to my right said,

"I'm burying my third brother. All five of us kids joined Special Forces. There are only two of us left. That's not the worst of it. My youngest brother just got alerted for Vietnam. He leaves in two weeks.  My mother doesn't know my other brother is dead yet, or that the youngest is leaving and will be next.  I won't tell her any of this until I get home with the body.  I'm afraid it's going to kill her."

How ironic, at this table, I was seeing both the worst and the best of escort duty.  I was sitting with both the scum of the Army and the most noble, not only performing his military duties, but his family obligations.  The images of these soldiers, one at each end of the spectrum, would stay in my mind and remain in my psyche.  At the mess hall I realized that escort duty was what one made of it.  I was determined not to dread it, but to perform my duties to the best of my ability, and in doing so, not cheapen but honor, not diminish, but memorialize Robert Wiedemann's death.

The death of SP5 Robert J. Wiedemann would come to play a major role in my life, drawing me to Vietnam and affecting many things I have done since my return.  This young man's death was a pivotal point in my military career, and over the years, he would become a friend – a friend I never knew.

**Flash-forward ►►  SF - O'Hare - Gary - 1 April 1968**

Several escorts and coffins were trucked to San Francisco International Airport.  After checking in, I was given special access to the tarmac.  As I saluted, I made sure that the coffin went up the baggage belt headfirst.  The "head first rule" insured that fluids didn't run to the upper portion of the body and distort the face, even though this was a closed casket. I was the last one to board the plane. Once in my seat, I didn't look at the passengers around me. I sat silently in my window-seat and didn't move. I was aware of stares in my direction. Passengers looking out their windows had seen me pay respects to Robert Wiedemann's coffin as it went up the baggage belt, and watched me remove my white gloves almost immediately after rendering the salute. When I had boarded the aircraft and walked down the aisle to my seat, it was as if being the last one to board, I was holding up the airplane's take-off. They knew I was escorting a fallen soldier home for burial, and they didn't like it any more than I did.

Arriving in Chicago, I was the first one off the plane. Chicago was cold in early April, really cold! The little *one-man-cab-elevator-truck* scurried across the airfield carrying Bobby's coffin on its open bed. I hung on to the strange little vehicle as the wind whipped across my face. I wanted to cover my ears with my hands, but I couldn't let go.

The coffin was placed in an unheated hangar, giving no respite from the cold, but some relief from the wind. Within minutes, a hearse with Indiana license plates backed into the hangar and two young men, wearing navy blue blazers, hopped out. They were about my age but were typical collegiate types who had never seen military service. The coffin was placed in the hearse and realizing that three of us would share the front seat, I maneuvered myself to get in last. I wanted to occupy the outside passenger seat closest to the right window.

The hearse pulled out of O'Hare Airport onto the highway leading to Gary. The heater was powerful. This was good. It was bitter cold outside.

"Did they feed you on the plane?" the driver asked.

"Just soda and peanuts," I replied.

Within minutes we were at a hamburger drive-thru.

*What a bizarre scene this must be to observers,* I thought.  It was my first guilty feeling that week, although I wasn't really responsible for the driver taking the body through the drive-thru.  I figured if I had kept my mouth shut and said, "Yes, I ate on the plane," we wouldn't have committed this act of misconduct.  This wasn't right.  It was really disrespectful to this soldier's memory.

"You don't have to pull in here to get food for me," I told the driver.

"We're not supposed to do this," he said, "but we didn't eat any lunch either."

"As long as we don't get caught," commented the other, "it's alright."

I declined ordering anything.  They didn't understand, but it was my way of protesting their actions.

"No, I don't want anything," I told them.

The limousine went silent.

The driver fumbled with the wrappers, eating his burger with one hand, and barely holding the steering wheel and fries with the other.

I was thinking about the dead soldier in the back, Specialist Robert J. Wiedemann, and how I knew him only as a name and a silver coffin. I didn't know him as "Bobby" then, and I wondered what he had looked like.

Suddenly, with a mouthful of food, the driver said, "You don't have anything to worry about, the Wiedemanns are white, and a very nice family. I'm sure they'll be relieved knowing you are white too."

Funny that he mentioned this, in such a way and just at this time. I was thinking about my briefing at Oakland when told that black families get black escorts and white families get white escorts. There were no guarantees, however. What if I had been black? I know the answer to that question now. My race wouldn't have made any difference, to the Wiedemanns, whatsoever.

*This black/white coffin switch thing must have hit the newspapers like a bombshell!* I thought.

As the driver wadded up his hamburger wrapper he said,

"The Wiedemanns want to open the casket and see the body. They'll be doing it in the morning."

Now, his comment hit me like a bombshell! *Oh shit,* I thought, *here comes the pitchfork!*

"You'll be staying at the funeral home.  You won't have to worry about getting a hotel.  Everything you need is right there," he added, as little pieces of his meal spewed from his mouth.

Spring hadn't yet arrived in Indiana.  I remember the winter grey of the city as the limousine approached Gary, and I thought how depressing it was.  Gary's drab veil just added to the shroud hanging over the funeral.  My duties were becoming more complicated – they were going to open Robert Wiedemann's coffin.  What were they going to find?

At the funeral home the casket was removed from the hearse, and went to the basement in a freight elevator.  I was shown to my room upstairs.  The ceilings on the first floor were so high that the staircase to the second floor was long, straight and foreboding.  I wished I had gotten a hotel room.

I was shown up the staircase and into the room.  I threw my gear on the bed and tried to settle in, but thought about the stiffs I had just seen displayed on the first floor.  They were hard not to notice when I entered.  I didn't want to stay in this room any more than necessary.  Although the smell of flowers wafted up to the second floor, there was also a sterile hospital smell, the odor of formaldehyde or witch-hazel.  *Snap out of it,* I told myself, *you're dwelling on nothing but morbid thoughts.*

There were no curtains or pictures in the room, just one small window that looked out on the alley.  The bottom half was frosted glass.  I made a point of standing on my toes and craning my neck to look out to get my bearings, but the alley below gave no clues,  revealing instead just a few over-flowing trashcans waiting for pick-up.  In the room, there was a writing desk against the wall and an old wooden chair.  The rug was burgundy and was frayed on the corner nearest the door leading to the stairs.  The bedspread was made from long, flat, brown and straw colored strips of fabric, woven together.  It looked like a giant potholder.  At least the sheets on the bed were clean.

I changed into civvies and walked downstairs to hear voices in the basement.  I thought nothing of them at the time, and walked a few blocks into town, finding a one-screen movie house, where *Valley of the Dolls* was showing.  I always pay attention at the movies, but drifted in and out of this one, thinking about the last twenty-four hours.  *Valley of the Dolls* will forever be associated with *my* Vietnam experience, but at the time I didn't know why.

It's strange, how movies can be identified with actual events. The first two names inscribed on the Vietnam Veterans Memorial in Washington, DC, Dale Buis and Chester Ovnand, were killed at a converted saw mill at Bien Hoa, 5 July 1959, while watching, *The Tattered Dress,* starring Jean Crane and Jeff Chandler.  As they watched the movie the Viet Cong stuck a MAT-50 French machine-gun through an opened window and gunned them down.

US Marine Corps, Major Donald Koelper's death is likewise tied to a movie, *The List of Adrian Messenger,* which played at the Kinh Do Movie Theatre in Saigon on 16 February 1964. Discovering VC sappers in the lobby, Don attempted to wrestle a satchel charge away from one of the enemy when the charge exploded.

Within a year of the Wiedemann funeral, in addition to *Valley of the Dolls*, there would be three other movies forever associated with *my* Vietnam – *Jigsaw,* starring Harry Gardino, *Rage,* starring Glenn Ford and *The Killers,* starring Lee Marvin.

### Flash-forward  ▶▶  Cu Chi, SVN – 28 February 1969

For three consecutive nights, after the second reel of *Jigsaw*, the movie was interrupted by NVA attacks on the base camp at Cu Chi.  We would hit the fence line for its defense and never see the end of the movie.  On the last night that *Jigsaw* played at Cu Chi, my best friend in Vietnam, SP4 Ben Barrett and I, after spending a day at Long Binh, raced thirty-plus miles from Dian (pronounced zee-on) to Cu Chi in the pitch black, through night time enemy territory, so as not to miss the end of *Jigsaw* a fourth night in a row.

At age twenty-three in a combat zone, your priorities are skewed and you feel indestructible.  Being both foolhardy and downright stupid, for me, seeing the end of *Jigsaw* was more important than life itself.

The Bronze Star Medal, I received in Vietnam, was not for an act of valor, it was however, for doing several things right, by my count, averaging one situation a month. This irresponsibility on my part, getting back to see *Jigsaw*, running the roads in the pitch black without  black-out lights; crossing two US guarded bridges in the middle of the night, was not one of them.

We might have been ambushed by the Viet Cong or killed by our own guys guarding the bridges. How senseless! I put Ben's life in danger over a movie. I was the ranking man and I should have known better.

### ◄◄ Rewind, Camp Davies, SVN – July 1968

The movie, *Rage,* starring Glenn Ford was the last movie I had seen stateside, while on leave in May 1968. Now, tame by today's standards, *Rage* was an edge of your seat thriller, about a German Shepherd that contracts rabies and infects a local migrant worker who, tied to a pole, is reduced to less than human as he lives out his final rage. The rest of the movie, Glenn Ford running for his life to get anti-rabies serum, didn't seem to matter much, but the movie stuck in my mind.

I had never seen an animal or a person with rabies, and the movie's special effects seemed quite realistic. Those images had been put on a backburner, until July 1968, while on patrol, they resurfaced as I drove my jeep onto Camp Davies near Saigon. There, I spotted a small terrier with giant black scabs on its hindquarters. It was dragging its back left leg, foaming at the mouth and having a hard time breathing.

Stopping my jeep a respectable distance, I hopped out grabbing my M-1 carbine, which lay between the two front seats. M-1 carbines weren't standard issue in Vietnam. This was an outdated weapon I had inherited along with jeep SSC-TMP7, when I took over the function of patrolling Cholon, the Chinese district of Saigon.

"Griffin," I said to the soldier with me, "get behind the wheel. Go back to the main gate and bring back one of the MPs manning the guard shack."

"For what, Sarge?" he replied.

"Dog's got rabies," I said.

"How do you know that?" he asked.

Bad move to tell the truth, but I blurted out, "I know he has rabies, because I saw it in a Glenn Ford movie."

"Sarge, you got to be kidding?" he responded.

"Griffin, just go get the fucking MP!" I demanded.

He disappeared down the road, as I watched the dog continue to limp across the lawn.  The animal was getting close to some Quonset huts across the street from the Camp Davies NCO Club, and I knew it was almost noontime – lunchtime.  I wondered what I would do, if suddenly the dog were among a group of soldiers.

*I'd have to shoot it myself,* I thought, *and there'd be Hell to pay.*

Griffin returned in the jeep, followed by an MP driving another jeep with 716 MP markings.  From the front, the jeeps looked similar.  One jeep had black letters on a white background below the windshield, reading MOVEMENTS CONTROL, the other read, MILITARY POLICE.

"What seems to be the trouble, Sarge?" the MP asked.

"This dog's got rabies. You'll have to shoot it," I replied with my eyes transfixed on the rabid dog.

"I can't discharge a firearm on post, Sarge. How do you know it has rabies?"

"I know the dog has rabies 'cause I saw it in a Glenn Ford movie," *Damn! I did it again!*

"Sarge, I don't have time for this. I have to get back to my post."

The MP swung into his jeep, did a U-turn and disappeared down the road to the main gate, without taking any action.

"Come on, Sarge. Leave the dog," said Griffin.

I already figured I'd be dancing with the devil for discharging my M-1 carbine on Camp Davies, but I knew I was right to do so. I approached the dog, within ten or twelve feet, and fired a single bullet into the dog's chest. It collapsed to its right. The gurgling chest had made a better target than the dog's head – luckily for me. Shooting a rabid dog in the brain only complicates things, or so I have been told. I made certain that if the round went through the dog it would lodge in the grass. No one was interested in my explanation. When I fired, dozens of soldiers and officers came out of surrounding Quonset huts. The scene was chaotic except for the three little Vietnamese women sitting in the noon day sun under their conical bamboo hats, looking on in silent curiosity.

"Did you fire that shot, Sergeant?" a tall, swashbuckling major with a pencil thin moustache asked redundantly.

*I'm the only one standing here with a weapon in my hand,* I thought.

"Yes, Sir, I shot the dog. It had rabies."

He gestured for me to hand him the weapon. I removed the clip and cleared the round in the chamber. I could see even this action made him really nervous. He was a *chair-borne admin type;* tied to a desk at Camp Davies. I held the clip in my left hand. He held my weapon in his right. He was about six foot four, and so tall, he looked silly holding that little M-1 carbine.

"How do you know the dog has rabies, Sergeant?"

If I had lived on a farm in North Carolina, I could have made up some story about how my Granddaddy had shot a rabid dog when I was a kid, or how rabid raccoons got into the chicken house. Anything was more believable than what I told him.

"Sir, this dog has rabies. While I was on leave coming over here, I saw a rabid dog in a Glenn Ford movie. It was entitled *Rage*."

He looked so damned smug as a cocky little sneer materialized below his silly little moustache. I was in deep shit now. I could see nothing I could say was going to work.

"Stand at parade rest, Sergeant."

I assumed the position as ordered. I stood in the sun for half an hour while the major contacted the veterinarians at Saigon Port. They took their sweet time getting there. When they arrived, the major was still staring in my direction, talking to his superiors and subordinates in whispers. It was clear to me that he was making it appear as though *he*, not I, had brought the situation under control.

After a brief huddle with the veterinarians, meat inspectors from Saigon Port, the major approached me with all the saunter and pomp he could muster. Behind him, the now gloved veterinarians were placing the dog's body in a black plastic bag.

"Sergeant, you can go now," he said, exhibiting his right as an officer.

He handed me my weapon, the way people shake your hand when they really don't want to.

"Well, Major, did the dog have rabies?"

He wouldn't answer my question.  I couldn't believe it.  I asked him again.

"You heard me, Sergeant.   You can go now.   You're dismissed."

He wouldn't confirm that the dog had rabies.   There was no "Thank you."  There was no, "Sergeant, job well done," just a simple dismissal.

I knew that I had done the right thing.  I had overheard the veterinarians confirm that the terrier had rabies.  I wanted to hear it from the major though, but I wasn't going to.  I knew I did what I did, because I recognized a rabid dog when I saw one.  I had seen one in a Glenn Ford movie, and now, I had seen one for real.

◄◄   **Rewind, Gary, Indiana – 2 April 1968**

I woke at 0730 hours, after an extremely restless night.  I found myself thrashing around and wrestling with the bed covers in my loft above the funeral parlor. Bobby Wiedemann's father was due here at 1000 hours.  I read, and re-read my instructions. It was his decision, and his alone, to open the coffin and view his son's remains.  I was obligated to give him my pre-hashed speech, then, let him have final say.

I made sure my uniform and shoes were perfect, and squared off my saucer cap.  I walked toward the movie theatre.  There was a diner in this direction for breakfast.  I was starved.

Like on the airplane getting here, I received stares at the diner, as if no one in Gary ever saw a soldier, on escort duty, wearing a black armband before.  Someone at the service bar asked what its significance was.  I could tell everyone within earshot was listening.  I tried to keep my answer short and to the point.  I could see the town of Gary wasn't ready for dead soldiers coming home in boxes.  There would be a lot more military funerals before Vietnam was over.  Indiana  lost 1,532 soldiers, sailors,  airmen and  Marines to the Vietnam War. The town of Gary lost 91 of its sons, 6 per cent of the state's total dead.

In 1989, at a Kokomo Vietnam veterans reunion, I learned about another of Gary's sons killed in Vietnam. PFC Joel Mock, USMC, lost his life on 21 March 1967.  Years later, unlike my unsuccessful search for veterans who knew Robert Wiedemann, I located Ron Bladt, who was with Mock, and obtained the inside story of their time at Dong Ha. *

The weather this morning in Gary was pleasant.  It was a big change from the day of my arrival in Chicago.  Back at the funeral home, I stood in the foyer next to the director.  He was a bald, immaculate little man wearing a suit.  I had a feeling that somehow I couldn't trust him.

* See Joel Mock's story beginning on page 104.

We looked out of the open doorway and watched Mr. Chester Wiedemann and his oldest surviving son, Bill, pull up in their sedan. Mr. Wiedemann was dressed in a plaid shirt, a pair of brown-cuffed pants and a brown leather belt too thin for its loops. He wore horn-rimmed bifocals. The strain of the war was already written in lines on his face. Bill, dressed for school, would be dropped off to continue his afternoon classes, once he viewed his older brother's remains.

"Good morning," said Mr. Wiedemann, "you must be the military escort."

"Yes, Sir, It's an honor to meet you."

"You know I intend to open my son's coffin, don't you, Sergeant?"

"Yes, Sir, I understand, and I've been instructed to advise you that the final decision is yours. However, I have also been instructed to tell you that the responsible individuals at the Department of the Army have made every effort to identify the remains as those of your son. They feel it is futile for you to break the seal on the coffin and view the deceased."

"You know, there was a body switched in the Chicago area a few weeks ago?" said Mr. Wiedemann. "There's nothing you or the Army can say to change my mind. I must know that we are burying my son. I have to bury Bobby and not someone else. I cannot put him in the ground without being certain he is mine. You understand, don't you, Sergeant?"

"Yes, Sir, I understand. The decision is yours."

"Did you know Bobby?  Were you stationed with him?"

"No, Sir, I wasn't."

"You didn't come with him from Vietnam?"

"No, Sir, I didn't. I'm stationed at Fort Leonard Wood, Missouri and flew out to meet his body in California."

"Do you know what our Bobby looked like?"

"No, Sir, I don't."

Mr. Wiedemann reached into his pocket and pulled out his son's basic training photo. There, on the 3" x 5" photograph was the head and shoulders of a young eighteen-year old kid, neither smiling, nor frowning, just looking into the camera. He was a good-looking boy with a round face, and close cropped dark hair.  He had dark eyebrows and friendly, yet piercing eyes. Mr. Wiedemann handed me the photograph and I studied it briefly without saying a word.  I tightened and drew in my lips in a half smile, half frown, and handed the photograph back to him.

I thought, *So, this is what he looked like.*

I wanted to say something like, "He looks like a fine, young man."

But then I didn't know whether to use the word *looks* or *looked*. Then I wanted to say,

"I bet you're really proud of him," but I refrained from that cliché as well.

Just then, the funeral director touched me on the shoulder and took Mr. Wiedemann by the arm and said,

"It's time for us to go downstairs and view the body."

We walked down the staircase into the basement and down a hallway with cubicle doors and frosted glass windows. We stood in front of the last door on the right. The funeral director paused to get our attention. It was then that I realized the seal on the coffin had been broken the night before, while I was at the movie watching *Valley of the Dolls*.

"The Army has done an excellent job of preparing your son for burial. Why don't we go in?" said the funeral director, as he pushed open a wooden framed, frosted glass door. The room was no bigger than twelve by fifteen feet. The coffin sat in the middle of the room, elevated on a collapsible aluminum platform. The smell of antiseptic hung heavily in the room. As I entered, the head of the coffin was to my right, the foot to my left. I sidestepped and once through the door I positioned myself at parade rest with my hands clutched behind my back. Unlike the rabid dog incident, five months later, at Camp Davies, I assumed this position without command. My semi-ridged stance seemed appropriate.

In the coffin there were two bags. The first was clear plastic and in it, I saw a Class-A uniform cleaned and pressed with Military Intelligence, US enlisted brass, and six military ribbons properly affixed. The uniform bore a large, gallant, golden

1$^{st}$ Cavalry Division patch on the shoulder. How many times have I heard, "the horse they never rode, the line they never crossed..." What a crock of bullshit. The 1$^{st}$ Cavalry patch has always been one of the proudest and most desirable emblems in the United States Army. None is bigger. None is bolder. SP5 Wiedemann's uniform carried it proudly.

The uniform looked as though it was ready for wear, as if it had just come back from the dry cleaners. Obviously, Robert Wiedemann would never have the occasion to wear it again. We stood in silence as the funeral director lifted the uniform and hung it on a hook in the corner of the room, exposing Robert Wiedemann in an open black bag, wrapped in gauze. The funeral director made a fist and tapped on the thorax, shoulders, chest and head. "Nothing here," he said.

I realized that all the areas he tapped on were constructed of plaster and only the bottom two thirds of Bobby's body was in the casket. Robert Wiedemann had somehow been cut almost in half. I didn't want to be in the room. I was feeling ill. I wanted to excuse myself and go outside. But, then I thought,

*No, I won't do it. My duty is to prevail. This isn't about me. This is about a fellow soldier, even though I never knew him, and about his acceptance by his family. My job is to remain here and do what I am supposed to do.*

The United States Army's forensic specialists had built a head, neck, shoulders and arms for Robert Wiedemann. Representation of his arms, crossed over his heart were reminiscent of one of King Arthur's knights or a fallen Holy Lands Crusader. The manner in which his body was posed was suggestive of images in bas-relief inscribed on ancient coffin covers, the kind that tourists travel to Europe to make brass rubbings of. Wrapped in gauze, his face exhibited no details, as if Claude Rains had posed for his facial features during the 1933 movie classic, *The Invisible Man*. The scene was neat and orderly – sterile, and impersonal.

Mr. Wiedemann placed his hands on the lower part of his son's chest, the part that still existed, the area that was actually flesh and bone.

"Bobby had a barrel chest," he said. "It appears that I'm feeling part of a barrel chest here," he added.

Then, Mr. Wiedemann examined the feet, first the right, and then the left. He spread the toes and looked at the bottoms of them. At that moment I thought about the conviction he was exhibiting. Then he rubbed them with his hands as he closed his eyes and paused for a moment. He looked at Bill, then at the funeral director, then at me.

"This is my son," he said, "this is Bobby."

Then he looked at Bill again, "This *is* your brother," he said, "Bobby has come home."

Bill had been standing at the head of the casket. Now, he walked along the far wall to the foot of the casket where his father was standing and gave his Dad a hug.

I had wanted to leave the room before, for my own selfish reasons. I just hadn't wanted to see a dead soldier. But now,

I realized I had to leave the room.  Not for my own self-centered reasons, but for the sake of the family.  At that moment, standing there at parade rest, looming over Bobby Wiedemann's coffin, I represented the military in its purest form, and I saw my presence as neither required nor desired. These were the last moments Mr. Wiedemann would ever spend with his son and for me to be there contributed nothing.  On the contrary, it detracted from it.  It was the military that had brought these circumstances to this end and no one in that room needed to be reminded of that.  I deemed my presence mute, overshadowing, unwanted and obscene.

"Sir, I'll be outside in the hallway if you need me." I opened the door and exited silently.  I stood outside the room at parade rest as if guarding the doorway.  I could hear shreds of the conversation going on beyond the wall behind me.  The time I stood there in the hallway also seemed like an eternity.

Finally, Mr. Wiedemann, Bill, and the funeral director exited the room.  As we walked back upstairs, Mr. Wiedemann pulled a cloth handkerchief from his pocket and wiped his eyes.  I was amazed at his courage.  He had gone into the room with a mission, the mission of identifying his son, and, as best I could tell, shed no tears until it was all over.  I was truly amazed at his strength of character and admired this man that I had only met a half hour before.

When we arrived at the foyer, the survival assistance officer from Fort Sheridan, Illinois, the closest military installation to Gary, was standing there in Class-A uniform.  He apologized for being late, excusing his tardiness because of Chicago traffic.

He expected a briefing. The funeral director and Mr. Wiedemann apprised him of the events that had taken place in the basement, explaining that the casket was opened and Mr. Wiedemann was satisfied that the body was that of his son. The SAO looked surprised, but Mr. Wiedemann changed the subject indicating that he was pleased with having me as his son's military escort.

The conversation between Mr. Wiedemann and the SAO shed light on Bobby's death.

After attending Military Intelligence School at Fort Holibird, Maryland, Specialist Fifth Class Robert J. Wiedemann, departed for Vietnam on 18 June 1967. He was assigned to the 223d Aviation Battalion, part of the 1st Aviation Brigade in Qui Nhon, but was working out of his Military Occupational Specialty (MOS). Sometime in November 1967, he requested a transfer to the 191st Military Intelligence Detachment supporting the 1st Cavalry Division. After spending time at Landing Zone Two-Bits near Bong Son, his new unit deployed near the DMZ after the siege of Khe Sanh was declared ended. The 191st was responsible for document exploitation and enemy interrogation. When the 1st Cavalry relieved the Marines at Khe Sanh, the 191st set up their base of operations north of Camp Evans. On the night of 25 March 1968, as Bobby Wiedemann slept, a 122mm rocket landed directly on him, destroying the upper one third of his body. We were told by the SAO that Bobby was killed in his sleep and never knew what hit him.

One thing that was noticeable, but has never been mentioned until now, is that whomever prepared Bobby's uniform for inclusion in his casket never knew he was also authorized a 1st Aviation Brigade patch as an alternate insignia on his upper right sleeve. He had served with the unit for the first half of his Vietnam tour!

### Flash-forward ►► Saigon, SVN – 11 June 1968

By the time I arrived in Vietnam the Tet-Offensive was over, and the enemy's new mission was to drop a hundred rockets a day into Saigon for a hundred days. Although, much of this was propaganda, the Viet Cong managed to smuggle a half-dozen rockets into the city daily. The rockets were launched each night and early morning from courtyards within the city. They crashed down blocks away causing isolated, yet, extensive destruction. Psychologically, this continued to terrorize the residents of Saigon, long after the Tet-Offensive had ended.

Late on 11 June, I arrived in Saigon and spent my first night in the 4th Transportation Command enlisted billets, known as the Le Lai Hotel. The following morning, 12 June, a military bus with a Vietnamese bus driver waited at the hotel entrance. The bus was dedicated to transport new soldiers from the Le Lai, four blocks from the Central Market, to Headquarters at Saigon Port for in-processing. As the ranking man, I was assigned as group leader and was responsible for twelve soldiers. I was told the bus was to leave at 0730 hours and to have all my people on board before then. Once all twelve were accounted for, I told the bus driver,

"Come on, Papa-san, let's go."

"No, no," he told me, "we wait two more minutes."

I was sitting in the front right seat and reached over and closed the door with the handle mechanism. "No," I said, "everyone's on board, you leave now!"

The bus pulled away from the Le Lai, but before we traveled the first two hundred yards we heard the drone of a 122mm rocket. Even if we had recognized the sound of incoming, there was still nothing any of us could have done. The rocket hit mere feet behind the moving bus. With a deafening explosion, it threw the back end on a 35-degree angle into the air. The bus hovered momentarily, balancing on its front wheels and bumper before the rear end came crashing back down. The bus' ass end was torn to shreds. The rocket had chewed up steel and duffel-bags stacked in the back. We were shaken up, but miraculously, no one was hurt. The duffel-bags had acted as sand bags and had taken the brunt of the shrapnel.

Another morning, a rocket blew a hole in the traffic circle by the Hoa Lui Hotel. At the time, I was in the Le Lai's elevator on my way to the ground floor. Six or seven rockets a day could seem like a hundred. Particularly, when they did real damage, as did two landing in the railroad yard across the street, which killed dozens of refugees living in boxcars. The carnage was tremendous and the psychological effects devastating.

Most nights in Saigon, I'd fall asleep exhausted, convinced that like Bobby Wiedemann, I'd be cut in two by a randomly aimed 122mm rocket. Each dawn, when I awoke, it was with disbelief that I was still alive. It was like being reborn every morning. The events leading up to my arrival in country had convinced me that I'd be killed some time between dusk and dawn.

Rocket attacks continued in Saigon through 22 August 1968, killing eighteen and wounding fifty-nine South Vietnamese civilians on that last day. The communists were aiming at the Le Lai Hotel, but somehow they never managed to hit it.

## ◄◄ Rewind, Gary, Indiana – 2 April 1968

Mr. Wiedemann invited both the survival assistance officer and myself for dinner at his home that evening. The SAO declined, saying he had duties back at Fort Sheridan. Before he left, he answered a few more questions that Mr. Wiedemann had. The SAO said he would return on the day of the funeral. Bobby's dad turned in my direction, and again invited me to dinner. I accepted.

At 1700 hours, Mr. Wiedemann picked me up at the funeral home and drove me to 400 Grant Street. It was a wooden, two-story, mission style house, probably built in the 1920s. There was a well-manicured lawn, a stainless steel fence and gate. We climbed half a dozen steps to the front door, entering the living room. Beyond it was a dining room, and at the end of the house was the kitchen. All the bedrooms seemed to be on the second floor. At the front of the house, to the left, was a sitting parlor. The interior was decorated with its fair share of antique furniture, plants and ferns. A large representation of Jesus on a crucifix hung on the wall. It was then apparent to me that the Wiedemanns were Roman Catholic.

*Oh Shit,* I thought, *I was baptized a Methodist. Not only do I have to tell them I've never been to Vietnam, I'll also have to tell them I'm not Catholic.*

Unlike most families now-a-days, the Wiedemanns ate dinner together. Mrs. Lillian Wiedemann appeared to be about the same age as her husband. She was a sweet, quiet listener. Most of her conversation involved, "Would you like another roll?" – "Did you get enough green beans?" I thought she might have been in denial, not having witnessed what the three of us had seen that afternoon – her dead son lying in a coffin in the funeral home basement. I was pretty certain she hadn't yet accepted the fact that her son wasn't coming home.

Bobby's sister, Marilyn, at seventeen was a typical teenager, a sweet, attractive girl, who, on occasion smiled in my direction. Bobby's younger brother Bill, shook my hand and said,

"It's good to see you again."

I have often thought how mature Bill was for a fifteen year old.

The youngest son, Joe, at eight years old was talkative, always smiling and animated in his gestures. I had the impression that like Mrs. Wiedemann, Joe had no idea that he would never see his eldest brother again,

"He's gonna sit in Bobby's chair for supper, isn't he, Dad?"

Mr. Wiedemann assured Joe that I would. I felt humble to be sitting at the place of honor at the table. I couldn't help thinking that Bobby's body was back at the funeral home.

There, in the middle of the dining room was a table for six. Mr. Wiedemann sat at the head with his back to the door. I sat to his right, in Bobby's chair. Mrs. Wiedemann was at the other end, nearest the kitchen. Bill sat to my right and Joe directly across from me. Marilyn sat to Mrs. Wiedemann's right. We had either pot roast or chicken. I'm not sure which, but I do remember passing around bowls of food, and that the meal was delicious. It was a very homey scene, right out of a Norman Rockwell painting. Mr. Wiedemann handed me a bowl of food as he said,

"Sergeant, please take all you want."

The subject of religion came up, but only for a moment. When I told them I was a Methodist, Mrs. Wiedemann smiled and said, "Oh, that's nice." There seemed to be total acceptance of who I was.

When I arrived in uniform, I had stirred things up. Wearing the uniform in the presence of the family was one of my instructions and I was wearing Good Conduct and National Defense ribbons.

"Did my brother, Bobby, get those too?" Joe asked.

I half smiled and said,

"Oh, he got a lot more than these. He received the Purple Heart, the Good Conduct, the National Defense, the Vietnam Service, and two South Vietnamese medals, the Cross of Gallantry and the Vietnam Campaign. I only have two. Your brother was awarded six."

"What colors are they?" he asked.

"Just about every color in the rainbow except blue," I told Joe.

I realized that being from a steel mill town like Gary, the Wiedemann family had no point of reference to the military. Tonight, I was it.

"When Bobby came home from the Army, the last time we saw him," said Joe, "he had a uniform like yours, but he didn't have anything on it then.  He got all that stuff in Vietnam, didn't he?"

"Yes," I told the youngster.

Mr. Wiedemann asked me if I wanted a beer.

"No, thank you, Sir," I said politely.

"I thought all Army sergeants drank beer," he said.

"Normally, Sir, I do drink beer, but the Army instructed me that drinking any alcoholic beverage is prohibited until the funeral is over."

That's when Mr. Wiedemann said, "Well, what do you normally drink?"

"I've spent time in Europe.  I prefer German beer or Heineken," I replied.

"So, you have spent time overseas?" he asked.

"Yes, Sir, a year in Korea and three years in Europe."

"The whole family is curious about Vietnam. Do you know much about it?"

"No, Sir. In June 1964, as my tour in Korea drew to a close, I had the opportunity to go to Vietnam. I was told, 'If you like Korea, you'll love Vietnam,' but, my orders came down for Europe instead. I assume that Korea and Vietnam have some similarities except for the combat, and the weather."

"Where were you stationed in Europe?" Mr. Wiedemann asked.

"In Paris, France, until General De Gaulle threw out the US military. "

"I understand that Saigon is called the Paris of the Orient," said Mr. Wiedemann, "do you know much about Saigon?"

"No, sir, all I know about Vietnam is what my uncle wrote to me when he was with the First Cavalry Division in 1965. He wrote me a letter that I received in Paris. I wish, now, I had brought it with me. He put some dirt and grass in the envelope and I still have it, all intact, back at Fort Leonard Wood. He explained that he was stationed in and around An Khe, then Bong Son and 'the Oasis.'"

All these years later, I still have my copy of Uncle Paul's letter. It is a tribute to all the men who served with the First Cavalry Division in Vietnam.

*Hi Ray,*

*My tour of duty with the 1st Air Cavalry Division will soon come to an end and I'll be leaving for a three year tour in Japan.*

*I can't leave without a feeling of great pride having been a small part of this fine group of men we call "The First Team." The progress made here is probably the best example of American drive, ingenuity and hard work that can be found anywhere in the world. I'm not just referring to the stories of bravery, hardship, combat, and the many men of my unit who won't be coming home. That's only half the battle story! As I look out over the (Camp Radcliff) area, I see buildings everywhere; showers, orderly rooms, offices, clubs, day rooms, dispensaries, mess halls, chapels and more. Every ounce of cement laid, every nail driven, every board cut in every building, was built by the same GI's that fought in the Ia Drang, Pleiku and Bong Son. Less than half the materials used were issued through government channels, the rest was 'procured' by pure old American ingenuity. Talk about irony, our chapel roof is constructed from 105mm artillery ammo boxes, over 3,000 expended rounds worth.*

*Most other bases have Vietnamese house boys or Mama-sans, but since no Vietnamese nationals are allowed within the confines of the world's largest heliport here at An Khe, our men wash their own clothes, clean their own latrines, pull their own KP, carry their own garbage, haul their own water, run their own clubs, maintain their own PX's and clean their own tents - seven days a week, 365 days a year, and all between the fighting.*

*The day after "Operation Crazy Horse," a fiercely fought battle just outside our perimeter, the same men who fought, hauled eighteen truck loads of sand, to level an area for troop billets. The 2½ ton truck they used was loaded by the shovel full and unloaded the same way. It's hard to believe the young blond headed KP with soapy hands and dirty fatigues, who was washing pots and pans today, received the Silver Star a couple of days ago. The story behind the glory of the First Air Cavalry Division - one of sweat, calloused hands, tired backs and dirty details, is also a story of great fighting men. As we have progressed in war and in building Camp Radcliff so have we progressed in helping the Vietnamese people.*

*I went on the first combat operations of the "First Team" in Vinh Thinh Valley, known as "Happy Valley" in September and October 1965. It was a nest of VC. Death was behind every tree. It is ironic that on the 19th and 20th July 1966, I went back to Vinh Thinh Valley for "Operation Good Friend," which was to be my last.*

*Instead, of using weapons and ammo to fight our way in, we brought literature, food, clothing, a cultural entertainment group, the 1st Cavalry Band and a Vietnamese musical group. We pulled teeth, gave shots for prevention of disease, and taught personal hygiene.*

*We fed the three-thousand villagers a simple meal of chicken and rice, bread, jam, cookies and orange juice. Not knowing if they were going to get their share, they mobbed the serving lines, broke up equipment and over-ran the cooks in an attempt to get fed.*

*Nonetheless, we have progressed in the Central Highlands area, but there's still a big job ahead.*

*Certainly, all the fighting isn't over. Our replacements have been challenged to the same progress, and as I look at them reporting in, full of vigor, ambition and more ingenuity, I know that what the 1st Cavalry has done here is only the beginning. These hard working professionals, who first came over here, now weary and drained, are being replaced with new men who will take up where they left off.*

*I have scooped up a handful of dirt and dust, and am sending you a small piece of Vietnam.*

*God Bless, Uncle Paul*

Bobby Wiedemann was one of those replacements my Uncle spoke of. I conveyed the spirit of the letter, as best I could remember, to the Wiedemann family, as everyone at the table listened attentively.

Then, Joe asked about the animals in Vietnam. Specifically, about the bugs and snakes. I had no answer for him then, but had he asked the question a couple of years later, I could have told him about the six-inch-long, flying-cockroaches at Thu Duc, and the transparent, ant-like scorpions that roamed freely at Thu Duc's OK Corral. Had it been a couple of years later, I probably would have shared the story of the enormous beetle that was perched on top of my mosquito net one night. Writing a letter home, I had the impression that something was watching me. I turned to see the biggest, most bizarre, black beetle one could imagine. The hair stood up on the back of my neck. I rolled out of my bunk, as the beetle jumped off the mosquito net to challenge me. I beat it with my combat boot into a great, green-brown, wet stain on the plywood floor.

I'm sure Joe would have enjoyed the tale of the six-foot python that I traded with a Vietnamese youngster for a Timex watch, while monitoring a passing convoy. The kid was about Joe's age, and he presented the proposed pet in an oversized sandbag. Joe might have cringed if I had told him that our German Shepherd style mascot got too close to the snake, and quick as a whistle, it nearly strangled our pet. It took three of us to uncoil the snake from the dog, and just in the nick of time.

Joe probably would have laughed if I'd told him that I had posed with the python, for a photo, my arms extended, as I draped it over my shoulders. The photo was never snapped. The snake had taken a giant crap on my back, and I immediately set it on the ground so I could get my shirt off. The smell was unbearable! I would have told Joe how the snake lived for a time in my room and how it would curl up on my belly to keep warm at night. Joe would have enjoyed those anecdotes. But, of course,  I said none of this, because they hadn't happened yet.

"No, I'm sorry," I said, "I don't know anything about the bugs, snakes and critters in Vietnam."

Marilyn wanted to know more about how the people over there lived. All I could relate it to was the thatched-roof mud huts of Korea and told the teenager that they were similar to houses in documentaries about Africa.

"Rice paddies are everywhere," I said, speaking about Korea, but letting her assume I was talking about Vietnam. "The people have primitive tools and use oxen in the fields. In the cities they overload public transportation,  have bicycles instead of cars, and boys and girls don't wear pants until they're four or five years old."

The "no pants" part got a chuckle, and Joe chirped in with,

"How come they don't wear pants?"

"No diapers," I said. "They do their business wherever they stand!"

Bill asked about combat in Vietnam. The only thing I could relate to was my experience in Korea, when my unit, in combat gear and M-14 Rifles, marched through rice paddies near Camp Mercer. We walked on rice paddy dikes for three-hours. Somebody's idea of a training exercise. The connection was flawed. My trek through the rice paddies in Korea in no way prepared me for the reality of actual combat in Vietnam, nor could I have known the combat that Bobby had experienced.

## Flash-forward ▶▶   Cu Chi, SVN - 25 February 1969

If Bill had asked his question about combat years later, it is doubtful that I would have shared with him the events of the night of 25 February 1969, at least not until the year 2003.

The circumstances of that night in Vietnam have clawed away at me since, and I have only mentioned them when I meet other veterans who I am certain were at Cu Chi then. It is a time fixed and frozen in each of our memories.

Cu Chi Base Camp, Hau Nghia Province, was built in 1966, on the site of a former peanut plantation known by the Vietnamese as Dong Zu Base, which means "paratrooper's field." Cu Chi, the 25th Infantry Division's sprawling installation was surrounded by dense forest laced with a labyrinth of enemy tunnels. Contrary to popular belief, the enemy tunnels were not directly under the base camp, but rather to the north and northwest. The base camp was located twenty-five miles northwest of Saigon and just south of the Iron Triangle. To the north of the base was the Fil Hol Plantation, a former rubber plantation from which the Viet Cong would launch rocket attacks against the base. Further to the northwest were the Hobo Woods, a major stronghold and operating base of the Viet Cong and NVA. The area around Cu Chi was the scene of some of the most destructive operations of the war.

Cu Chi Base Camp, like the 90th Replacement Battalion's compound at Long Binh, had little vegetation, but unlike Long Binh's red clay, the earth at Cu Chi was a fine talcum-powder-like substance that resisted initial contact with water. I often watched the first drops of afternoon rain bead as they hit the ground and create miniature dust devils. In Cu Chi you could stand ass deep in mud and get dust in your eyes.

On 25 February 1969, twelve members of a North Vietnamese Army (NVA) demolition team breached Cu Chi Base Camp. Naked, except for satchel charges and weapons, the sappers negotiated a double apron, barbed wire fence, entering the camp undetected. The enemy soldiers walked into the showers of the 554th Engineers, and silently attacked the engineers who were removing grime from their bodies after spreading oil on the roads of Cu Chi Base Camp to keep the dust down.

Hand to hand combat is battle in its most primitive form.  This brief struggle, pitting the two groups of adversaries against each other, harks back to our primal beginnings.    Unclothed American soldiers fought for their lives against their naked enemy attackers.  The enemy had the advantage of surprise and weaponry.  Razor sharp knives were the ultimate weapons. Within minutes, the Americans were all dead.  The enemy left the showerheads running, washing away the blood of their victory.

Stealing GI shorts and cigarettes, the NVA sappers walked along the perimeter road to the 242d Aviation Company, the *Mule-Skinner* Helicopter Pad.  Tower guards saw them walking down the road, but talking and smoking on the friendly side of the wire, the guards didn't give them a second look.

The sappers sprang into CH-47 helicopters on the *Mule-Skinner* helipad, killing more US soldiers guarding the choppers, destroying eleven of fourteen of them on the pad.    The explosions were the signal for an all-out mortar attack, masking the fact that NVA regulars were loose on base.

We were watching the movie, *Jigsaw,* when all Hell broke loose.  We ran for the arms room, and then to the perimeter. Many of us were clad in sweatshirts, Levis' and shower shoes. We positioned ourselves behind 55-gallon drums spaced five feet apart, connected by walls of sandbags.  Beyond the drum and sandbag wall was a trench, then a road, another trench, a twelve-foot high barbed wire fence, rolls of concertina wire, and another twelve-foot high barbed wire fence.  Outside the perimeter, a flat, open area, containing claymores, extended towards the village  and the jungle.  The village side of  the base camp was not normally a free fire zone. Now, that didn't matter much. Our trek from the movie area, to the arms room, to the protection of the 55-gallon drums was chaotic. Thinking back to my second night in Vietnam, I remembered the painful experience of tearing off all ten toenails during that first attack.

There was no way I was going to repeat that experience. Here, I was almost barefoot in shower shoes. *I'm staying right here on the perimeter,* I thought, *this time I've got a weapon and I'm not running anywhere.*

We knew they were coming at us. We could hear shouts in Vietnamese and the sound of a commander's whistle. Any moment they would pour out of the jungle at us. I was here, but not really here. My mind was divorcing itself from my body. This wasn't time to think. It was time to react. We were ready for them.

Aerial flares were going off and between flares we were using our peripheral vision to see what was happening. When the flares went off, the light was so intense it burned my eyes. The flares floated to the ground on parachutes and would go out. That's when they'd advance again. We didn't know the enemy were regulars or that their NVA commanders had drugged them on opium, or maybe rice whiskey, or maybe just on patriotism. Later, we learned they buried their clothing and personal gear in long, shallow, slit trenches that wound through the jungle. Hiding their clothing concealed the designation of their units. As the waves of enemy got closer, we realized they were damned-near naked. The most fearful thing one can imagine, has to rate right up there with a charging NVA regular, on a dead run, coming right at you, AK-47 blazing, clad only in a loin cloth and covered with scabs and ring-worm. When we'd shoot them, sometimes even a solid hit seemed to have no effect and they kept coming. They had pre-tied strips of cloth around their arms and legs, and when they were hit, they would tighten down their tourniquets to stop the bleeding.

The first enemy out of the black jungle popped up in front of us as if from nowhere. Free Fire Zone or not, we fired on him, and like a basic training pop-up target, he dropped back down. He was hit. We could hear him screaming. Then, there was a shot from what sounded like a pistol and the screaming stopped.

When a flare went off, we'd pin point the enemy and everyone would fire on the same NVA soldiers. They'd disappear in big black stains. Intervals of bright light and pitch black allowed some NVA to get to the perimeter fence and climb the barbed wire. It didn't seem to bother them that the barbs were tearing their skin. A flare would go off as everybody fired at the same climbing enemy. As one flare burned out, another would illuminate the battlefield. Where moments before, a dead NVA soldier hung on the wire, now, only a hand, an arm and a shoulder were hanging there. We were chopping them to pieces.

There was so much more to the story. Thank God, they weren't things I could have told the Wiedemanns. It all happened exactly eleven months after Bobby's death. At Cu Chi, that night in February 1969, the NVA sappers were on base all night killing American soldiers, while beyond the perimeter they used one of our old bunkers against us. After action reports geared it all to 0445 hours, 26 February, Division commander, Major General Ellis W. Williamson and his staff played down the intensity of the attack and the fact that Cu Chi Base Camp had been taken by surprise.

According to John Fairbank who was the 25th ID Public Information Officer at the time, the first fire truck to respond to the burning *Mule-Skinner* helicopters struck one of the sappers as he crossed the road and killed him.  One can't help but think that sometimes justice goes beyond our understanding.

After daylight on the 26th my friend, Captain Ron Hunter, told me that a sapper was found digging under the laundry by the 2d Battalion, 34th Armor.  We arrived on site just in time to witness army engineers blowing the NVA soldier, and the laundry, straight to Hell.  We then policed the battlefield outside the perimeter, dumping dozens of NVA bodies, covered with lime, blood and stink, into the village of Cu Chi.  We still thought they were locals and figured their families would want their bodies.  The pile of dead remained untouched for a week, until 554th dozers dug a mass grave.  Their  families <u>were</u> waiting for them to return, but their families were waiting back in Hanoi.  When the shallow slit trenches that wound through the jungle were unearthed the diary of a North Vietnamese soldier, killed in the attack, was found.

> *3 January 1969 - for nearly sixteen days we have been sleeping in underground trenches without sunshine and oxygen which has resulted in us having itchy bodies. We have to contend with mosquitoes that are also a dangerous enemy. In this situation we miss our unit, our families, and our beloved North Vietnam.*

*9 January 1969 - The Dong Zu (Cu Chi) position is very important; it lies near big lines of communication and is a corridor to defend Saigon. This morning, enemy tanks swept our area from 0630 to 0800 hours. After the withdrawal of US troops, the enemy used aircraft to broadcast surrender appeals, threatening that he would drop bombs if we did not surrender.*

*25 January 1969 - My body is diseased by ringworm. We met no local inhabitants, we will have to go without food today.*

*7 February 1969 - I miss Luc and Hoa so much and perhaps Luc misses me too. Take courage, my darling.*

*25 February 1969 - Three months of hard preparation on the battlefield! Tonight, I, Assistant Arrow Leader, and Comrade Dau, Arrow Leader will lead our unit in launching an attack on the US position at Dong Zu.*

This NVA soldier, *Assistant Arrow Leader,* had a life, a family, and people he cared for, and people who cared for him. I have often wondered if his family ever knew his fate.

## ◀◀Rewind, 400 Grant Street, Gary, Indiana - 2 April 1968

I am grateful for that night in Gary when I showed my naiveté and ignorance. The Wiedemann family didn't deserve to hear stories like these. At the time, I felt guilty that their son had died in a far away land that I hadn't been to yet. I couldn't answer their questions about the sights, the sounds and the smells of Vietnam. I couldn't answer their questions about the attacks, the bullshit, the camaraderie we shared, the red Latterite clay, the choking blinding dust of convoys, the two o'clock monsoon rain, the crack of an AK-47, or about any of the other things their son might have experienced.

The kids wanted me to help clear the table, while the parents objected saying, "Sergeant Bows doesn't have to do that."

That's when young Joe said, "But, Daddy, Bobby used to help clear the table."

It was an honor to help. I obliged.

As I tried to do my part, I was thinking about what the SAO had said that afternoon. At his own request, Bobby had been transferred from the 223d Aviation Battalion in Qui Nhon to the 1st Cav's 191st Military Intelligence Battalion at Bong Son, which was a much more dangerous assignment. It was ironic that I had been transferred that same month from a cushy job as an advisor to an Army Reserve unit in Cheyenne, Wyoming to Fort "Lost in the Woods," Missouri. Why did Bobby do it? Why did I do it? Why does a soldier request a transfer into the Tiger's belly? My only answer is that it's about being unhappy and wanting to be someplace else.

*In February 1969, the enemy began a series of savage attacks on the villages and hamlets of Hau Nghia Province, but were roundly defeated by local South Vietnamese forces. Shown here two South Vietnamese Rangers return from battle.*

## Next Day – Funeral Home, Gary, Indiana – 3 April 1968

The next morning, I woke early and again got one of my Class-A uniforms ready for wear. I had brought two with me and was saving one specifically for the day of the funeral. I was downstairs before almost anyone else. By this time, Bobby Wiedemann's closed coffin was on display in one of the large parlors. There were dozens of floral displays left, right, and center. Many were of patriotic themes bearing ribbons reading "Our Hero" and "For a Fine Soldier." I bowed my head in silence.

Those coming to pay respects began trickling in, slowly at first, but as the morning progressed they came in greater numbers. Bobby's classmates from both grammar and high school, uncles, aunts and cousins, Mr. Wiedemann's fellow workers from the foundry, people from the local church, neighbors and friends of the family, some of Bobby's teachers and the local priest.

As I stood at the end of the receiving line, the introductions were never ending, and I was tiring of answering the same questions over and over.

"What was the significance of the armband?"

"No, I didn't know Bobby when he was alive."

"No, I haven't been to Vietnam."

It was bizarre, because amongst it all, the Wiedemanns, their family, friends and associates, were all trying to make me feel at home and at ease.   Somehow they seemed to sense the precarious position in which the Army had placed me.   Now, thirty-five years later, it's hard for me to separate my memories of Bobby's wake and funeral from my own memories and images of Vietnam.

**Flash-forward** ▶▶ **Le Lai Hotel, Saigon** – **10 June 1968**

When I arrived at the Le Lai, nobody wanted Room 45, on the fourth floor.   The room had a panoramic view of the railroad yard across the street, where all the refugees lived. Room 45 had been freshly painted and even the ceiling and floor seemed to have been scrubbed clean.   Although, it took me a few minutes to get used to the geckos running across the walls, I jumped at the opportunity to be quartered there.

I only served under the command of General William Westmoreland for four days.   On 10 June, General Creighton Abrams assumed command of all United States Forces in Vietnam from Westmoreland. That same day, I was hired as a bartender during my off duty hours at the club on the Le Lai's sixth floor.  Before the days of flip tops, I served cans of beer, rum or whiskey and Coke, Bloody Marys, and Screwdrivers. After ordering their drinks, some of the guys who had been around a while, would say something to the effect, "Oh, you're the one who's in Room 45." They'd smile or chuckle and walk off.  It took me a few days to learn Room 45's secret, even if it was only a secret to me.

During the Tet-Offensive, the Le Lai was known as "Old Ironsides." It's balconies on all floors enabled enlisted soldiers to position themselves with commanding vantage points from the Central Market, down to the dental clinic at the far end of the railroad yard, up the street to the Koelper Compound, and around the west face to the Hoa Lui Hotel. When the Viet Cong launched the Tet-Offensive, the Le Lai's US soldiers fired at anything and everything that moved. In the aftermath, there were dead dogs, cats and wounded civilians picked off by "Saigon Commandos" at the Le Lai. A military police patrol was pinned down behind a steel dumpster for four hours. And, all this was accomplished with the soon to be replaced M-14 Rifle.

Prior to Tet, one military stevedore who worked at Saigon Port frequented the bar upstairs each night, while rolling and fondling an M-14 projectile in his hand. He had misappropriated the 7.62 round during basic training. It was "his" bullet, maybe somewhere he had heard the poem, *Fiddler's Green.* *

> *...And in a roaring charge of fierce melee*
> *You stop a bullet clean,*
> *And the hostiles come to get your scalp,*
> *Just empty your canteen,*
> *And put a bullet to your head*
> *And go to Fiddler's Green.*

---

* For the entire poem, *Fiddler's Green,* see page 137.

On the first day of the 1968 Tet-Offensive, that stevedore, the occupant of Room 45, left the bar, walked downstairs to the fourth floor, locked and loaded the round into his M-14 Rifle, placed it under his chin, and splattered his brains all over the ceiling of Room 45.

### Flash-forward ►► Thu Duc, SVN – September 1968

Between, the Mexican War and 1855, the Army developed the first Buddy System.  Men were organized into "files" of two soldiers each, and were taught to stick together in a fight.  By the 1960's, during basic training, two man pup tents on Bivouac were the standard, and soldiers were always paired off during weapons qualification and other tasks and missions.

In Vietnam, lots of things seemed to come in twos.  There were two R & R s while in country; two cans of beer or soda a day for troops in the field; and two bridges to cross from Dian to Cu Chi.  When we ran the roads, it was deemed we pair off in twos.  It haunted me that one night, Ben Barrett and I had taken chances crossing those two bridges for the sake of watching the end of *Jigsaw*. We had missed it, not twice, but thrice.

I met SP4 Benjamin Barrett in September 1968, when I transferred to Thu Duc.  Ben, a year or two younger than I, was from West Virginia.  I quickly learned that he was quiet, level headed, loyal and was always ready to run the roads.  We became a team.  No matter the predicament, I knew I could count on Ben.  Ben volunteered to go from Thu Duc to Cu Chi with me.   He and I were often together, until towards the end of my tour, I landed him a transfer to Vung Tau.

While we were stationed at Thu Duc, on two different occasions, Ben and I picked up fragmentation grenades spotted on the Long Binh Highway, once in a jeep, once in an old shit box of an Equipment Incorporated pick-up truck.  The grenades carelessly dropped by their military owners, were not retrieved by simply making a U-turn on the highway as they could have been.  They were left for someone else to take care of.

On both occasions, pulling over to the side of the road, I envisioned some officer or some NCO saying to his driver,

"I just lost a grenade.  Let's keep moving before that thing goes off."

Our boss, Major Rochelle, would cringe every time Ben and I returned to Thu Duc, although, he only witnessed our grenade harvesting twice.  We were pretty nonchalant about the whole thing, both times we wrapped the grenades in my body armor and Ben held them on the floor of the vehicle with his feet so they wouldn't bounce around.

"Here come Bows and Barrett!  Wonder what they're bringing back this time?"

The pull-pin type fragmentation grenades came in twos, and by my reckoning so did soldiers who blew their heads off.  The second soldier I knew of, did not do it with an M-14, but with a self-arming M-79 grenade.  M-79 grenades, when fired, arm after a certain number of high speed rotations in the air.  If flipped in the air by hand, the arming wheel rotates a little with each and every spin. Just for something to do, one soldier stationed at Phu Loi, continually spun the same round, week after week, until the round armed itself, and like the bullet in Room 45, it blew his head off.

Finding our third grenade broke the rule of twos. It was a self-arming M-79, and Ben and I had already heard the *Don't spin an M-79 Grenade* story. There it was in the middle of the highway, spinning, twisting and turning as it glanced off one vehicle tire after another. We pulled our jeep to the side of the road. Ben flagged traffic away as I picked up the M-79 round, walked twenty or so steps to the side of the highway, and set down the projectile pointing up. We flagged down a 716th Military Police jeep headed north. I cautioned the MP driving, that the round was self-arming and was now his responsibility.

"Don't touch this thing," I told him. "Get on your radio and call EOD (Explosive Ordnance Disposal) and make sure that you stay clear of it."

As Ben and I drove off, I realized I recognized the MP. He was the same one who had ignored my request to shoot the rabid dog at Camp Davies.

"Ben, I know that guy," I said, "let me tell you a story. . . ."

### Flash-forward ►► Long Binh Highway – December 1968

On a warm morning in December 1968, after all three hand grenade incidents, Ben and I headed north to Long Binh. The Paris Peace Talks were all over the News, and Ben tried tuning in his transistor radio for the latest word on Armed Forces Radio. He was getting more static than news, when four miles north of Thu Duc we noticed elements of the 11th Armored Cavalry, in armored personnel carriers (APCs), dropping off the road and fanning out over dry rice paddies on a sweep. It was difficult to watch both track vehicles and the traffic ahead, while at the same time, Ben unrelentingly played with the radio's dial.

Within a mile, traffic locked to a stop. I executed an old Paris taxi driver's trick I learned while stationed there, and pulled into the oncoming lanes, which were free of traffic coming from the opposite direction. I passed as many vehicles as I could, doing it all illegally, as I advanced to the head of the three lanes by driving on the left. We had traveled three miles when we hit the Dong Nai Bridge. Soldiers had traffic locked down in both directions. One tried to wave us off, but I pulled around him.

"I think I've got the station, Sarge," Ben told me.

"Too late," I said, "something's going on here!"

"Looks like a fire, Sarge!"

Now, we were in the middle of the bridge, directly behind a five-ton stake and platform trailer (S&P), loaded with 105mm artillery rounds. The rear brakes had locked, and the left rear set of duels were smoldering.  Another soldier ran up asking if we had a fire extinguisher.

"We'll get one," I said, remembering the APCs down the road. I made a quick U-turn heading south towards the 11th Armored Cav's sweep.  They had to have fire extinguishers.  Within a mile, an MP from the 720th Military Police Battalion sat in his jeep on the crest of the hill monitoring traffic as he looked in our direction.  I whipped in to the little dirt parking area and shouted, "Do you have a fire extinguisher?"

"Yes, Sergeant, I do," he replied.

"Follow me!" I ordered, as we squealed back onto the road.  We passed civilian and military vehicles in a three abreast line as we traveled north in the left lanes.  In a couple of minutes we were on the bridge.

While Ben and I were gone, the situation on the bridge had worsened.  Now, there was an orange flame coming from the left hub, and the potential of the 105mm rounds exploding had increased.

Once we got there, the MP hesitated to hand me the extinguisher.  Realizing that he did not know how to operate it, I grabbed it from him, pulled the pin, and hit the handle. Nothing happened!  The damned thing was empty!

I looked to my right over the Dong Nai Bridge.  There was a barge site directly below us.  Ben stayed with our jeep, as I ran down the bridge for fifty yards, vaulted over the railing and dropped fifteen feet into the sand. I thought the sand would have cushioned my fall, but it felt like my neck had been driven into my pelvis. I ran to the little shack, which stood across the open, sandy area to the riverbank, and whipped open the screen door to find two NCOs sitting at a desk playing cards.

"There's a fire on the Bridge," I gasped, "do you have a fire extinguisher?"

The sergeant closest to the door looked in my direction, looked back at his opponent, and played his next card. Then, he pointed out the window.

"See that three-quarter-ton trailer down the beach? There's a fire extinguisher somewhere in it."

I headed for the trailer, which was five hundred yards away. It was hard running in the sand, my back ached, and I was out of breath, but had to keep going. Once there, the top of the trailer was chest high, so I untied one corner of the trailer's tarp jumping up and into it. Realizing it was three-quarters full of rusty, greasy water, I felt around until I located the extinguisher. Dragging it out, I threw it over my shoulder. It was full, two and a half feet long and as big around as one of my Aunt Fanny's dinner plates. I was slowing down. *Back through the sand, up the hill to the end of the bridge, and up the walkway,* I thought. Just then one of the NCOs, who had been playing cards, pulled next to me with his jeep, "Want a ride?" he asked.

When the sergeant got me to the bridge, we were blocked by traffic. I had to run the last few hundred yards with the extin-guisher over my shoulder. The S & P's back tires were in flames. Soldiers were on the trailer pulling away the tarp covering, trying to move 105mm boxes. Ben and I took turns spraying CO2. As the flames died, a fire truck from the Long Binh Fire Department showed up.

"Stand back," said a soldier from the fire truck, "we've got this under control!"

"Come on, Ben, let's go," I said. "Let's hit the NCO club and get lunch."

## ◄◄ Rewind, Funeral Home, Gary, Indiana – 3 April 1968

Many people were concerned that Bobby's casket was closed. Mr. Wiedemann side-stepped the issue. I picked up his lead. People didn't need to know the specifics of what had happened to Bobby's body. I haven't revealed the details until now.

Condolences were expressed. Periodically, family and friends knelt at the coffin and prayed. After two wake-sessions, Mr. Wiedemann put his hand on my shoulder saying,

"Sergeant, could you come back to the house again this evening for supper? Mrs. Wiedemann and I would be happy to have you as our guest again. You don't have to come in uniform and you can have a beer tonight, if you like."

"Compromise, Sir," I said, "Mrs. Wiedemann is a great cook and certainly, I'd like to come back to the house, but I must do so in uniform, and under no circumstances can I drink."

The funeral director closed one of the double doors of the parlor where Bobby's body lay. Soon the remaining mourners lingering or still paying their respects exited.

I returned with the Wiedemanns to their home. We sat around waiting for Mrs. Wiedemann to prepare supper, as eight-year old Joe approached me,

"Will you tell us another story about Vietnam tonight?"

"Joe," I said, "I've never been to Vietnam. I can tell you about Korea and Paris, or Frankfurt and London, but not Vietnam."

"Those places you've just said, do they have war there too?" Joe asked inquisitively.

I had known for several months, that in order to return to Europe, I needed to volunteer for Vietnam first. I had already volunteered for a second tour to Korea. The request had been disapproved. The Army had also denied me a short tour to the Middle East. We had troops stationed in Tehran, Iran then, but they didn't need me either. Now, I felt I had some real motivation for volunteering for Vietnam. Never again, did I want to be placed in a position like this. Not even by an eight year old. The thought of not being able to answer his questions about Vietnam was repulsive to me. Joe and the rest of the family had a right to have their questions answered.

I thought, *What the Hell is wrong with the United States Army that they couldn't find someone more qualified than me to be here? The Wiedemanns deserved better than this, they've lost their son.*

In peacetime, sons bury fathers.  In wartime, fathers bury sons.

I had lost my grandfather in 1964, while stationed in Korea, and was deeply saddened by the event.  Grandpa Bows was sixty-two when he died of a stroke.  When I was a kid, working for him, we sometimes had an adversarial relationship.  He had taught me a lot about work ethic, trying to instill in me the same principles that had inadvertently driven his own sons from him.  My Uncle Don wasn't the first to quit my grandfather's shoe business, nor was my Uncle Paul who joined the Army, making it a career to avoid working for his father.  Grandpa Bows was the only person, up to that point in my life, that I had ever lost, except for his son, my father, Clint, who had, because of pressure from my Grandfather, run off when I was four.

I couldn't imagine what it must have been like for Mr. Wiedemann to lose his son so young.  The Wiedemanns were all holding up extremely well.  Yet, it seemed as though one of their main concerns was making me feel at home.  I appreciated and respected each one of them for that.

We took our places at the table saying Grace and a prayer for Bobby.  Mr. Wiedemann started the prayer.  It went around the table clockwise with thoughtful words.  I knew the prayers were coming in my direction and it would be my turn to say something.  There was a pause…then I said,

"God Bless Bobby, and all the soldiers who are serving in Vietnam."

Mr. Wiedemann concluded with,

"…and God Bless Sergeant Bows who has been sent to us. In the name of the Father, and the Son, and the Holy Ghost, Amen."

It felt strange to be mentioned in their prayers. I felt humble and inadequate.

It was all soon forgotten.

We passed round bowls of food, dug in and ate. Mrs. Wiedemann was a great cook. I couldn't get enough of her food, but I didn't want to make a pig of myself. Even before the food was put on Joe's plate, the inquisitive youngster began pumping me with questions.

"Hey, Joe, slow down! I'll try to answer your questions, if I can, but one question at a time is all I can handle!"

He took a deep breath and one question came out.

"What kind of things happened in Vietnam?" he asked. "When you watch it on TV you only see soldiers shooting in the jungle. Dad said Bobby died in his bed."

Then the barrage continued,

"What kind of beds do they have over there? What kind of other things happened in Vietnam? What's it like to be in combat?"

My one-year tour in Korea was my only point of reference then, but now, there is so much more I could have told him.

**Flash-forward**  ►►  **Le Lai Hotel, Saigon – 27 June 1968**

After settling in Room 45, I was assigned duties with the Movements Control Center at Saigon Port. A few days later, on the day it was announced that the US Marines had begun the evacuation of Khe Sanh, I drew duty as sergeant of the guard at the Le Lai Hotel.

After curfew, one of my guards on duty at the entrance sent word that I was needed out front. There was commotion down the street and a woman was screaming. I grabbed my M-14, stuck the butt on my hip, and slowly walked a half block down the dimly lit street. Totally oblivious to any danger, I had no idea what I was getting in to.

Across from the railroad yard near the Koelper Compound, a Vietnamese husband was beating his wife. I grabbed him by the scruff of his neck and hauled him back to the Le Lai. As I dragged him away his wife screamed in his defense. She pleaded with me in Vietnamese not to take him. I ignored her and marched him down the street. At the Le Lai, under the stairs in the lobby was an empty closet. I opened the door and pushed him in, locking the door behind him. I was figuring by dawn he would behave himself. Once inside, he started pounding on the door. I opened it, told him in French to behave himself and shook him around a bit. Looking back on the incident, I wonder if I hadn't simply created another Viet Cong.

**Flash-forward ►► Saigon Port, SVN - 12 August 1968**

I was selected for other duties while at the Le Lai.  Colonel C. E. McCandless succeeded Colonel DeWitt C. Howell as CO of the 4th Transportation Command.  The change of command ceremony took place at Saigon Port, Headquarters Dock, 12 August 1968.  I was part of the color guard, carrying the 4th Transportation Command flag, bearing streamers dating back to World War II.  The 4th Trans. was a port headquarters during that war and had been recognized for campaigns in Normandy and Northern France.  It received one meritorious unit commendation in WWII, and later, two in Vietnam.

During Tet, Colonel McCandless earned a Bronze Star with "V" device for the defense of the Newport Terminal, and, was then selected to head the entire command.

The following month, with twenty months in grade, I was recommended for promotion to Sergeant First Class.  When I reported to the promotion board's Quonset hut at Headquarters Dock, a sergeant major on the board called me outside explaining, although I met the time in grade requirement, the command had overlooked that I did not have enough time in the Army for promotion to SFC.  I returned to my unit disappointed and a little bewildered.  When I got back and told my NCOIC, whose name I will not mention, what had happened, he said,

"No sweat, Bows.  Extend in Nam six months, and I guarantee you'll be promoted."

He was a  Saigon "village rat"  who had been in Nam for three years, reportedly with a wife and kids back in the states.

"Screw you, you desk jockey." I said underneath my breath. "I'll make SFC at my next duty assignment."

Shortly, after that Griffin and I ended up on night shift. Night shift was restricted to little more than patrolling the immediate Saigon Port area. We were under the supervision of one Master Sergeant Wilson who was doing nothing more than biding time and waiting for retirement. Griffin buddied up with a SP4 Bryant who was a smart-ass loud mouth. Within a couple of weeks I caught Griffin and Bryant drinking on duty as they buzzed around Saigon Port in one of our movement control jeeps. I locked their heels and proceeded to chew their asses.

Bryant interrupted me saying, "Fuck you, Sarge. Master Sergeant Wilson said we could break open a case of beer."

"Bryant, if what you are telling me is true, I'll have Master Sergeant Wilson, and your smart little mouth, in front of the commander in the morning."

Bryant ran to Wilson who must've been shaking in his boots. Before dawn I was transferred to Thu Duc. Wilson had an old Korean War buddy who was the NCOIC of the Thu Duc operation. I was isolated in the office of the Equipment Incorporated Trucking Company "checking trip tickets" from 0600 hours until 1800 hours. This lasted for three weeks until reporting the Griffin/Bryant drinking incident would have lost its impact.

I had heard the thunder of the drums and volunteered for Vietnam. I don't really know what I expected my tour to be like, but this wasn't it.

I had forgotten the actual dates of the ceremony, the disappointing promotion board and my abrupt transfer to Thu Duc for thirty-five years, until a 4th Transportation Command SHIP 'N SHORE NEWSLETTER jogged my memory on the date of the ceremony, and put these episodes in perspective for me. That same newsletter indicated the date the 4th Trans abandoned the Le Lai Hotel for new facilities at Camp Davies.

*"Every effort was made to improve troop living conditions. To that end, Camp Davies, just south of Saigon, became the operational responsibility of the 4th TC in November. Already home of provisional Harbor-Craft Company troops, the well-equipped and modern facility established by the 506th Field Depot, became the new location for Headquarters and Headquarters Company 4th TC in September. The troops made an orderly transfer of bag and baggage from the Le Lai Hotel in Saigon with no appreciable loss of operational efficiency."*

Perhaps, Colonel McCandless, and his staff, felt there was no appreciable loss of operational efficiency, but the enlisted men living at "Old Ironsides" were not happy about the move. Before my transfer to Thu Duc, we had gone from a "swanky" hotel with spacious rooms, cool breezes and an NCO club, the envy of any unit in Vietnam, to being crammed into Quonset-hut-cubicles with barely enough room to move around. We were bumping into each other and some guys were edgy. One of the military stevedores who had been billeted next to me worked on Quai-Docks at Saigon Port. He told me he was fed up with Vietnamese dock workers stealing and pilfering cargo.

"The next time I catch one bent over stealing," he said, "I'm going to slap him in the ass with a 'two by four.'"

Days later, he did, knocking the Vietnamese dock worker off the quai, into the Saigon River, among floating rubbish and garbage. To reverse his actions and save the drowning man, the stevedore dove over the side of the quai. Coming up for air, he kicked off the edge of the wall and again dove through the debris in an effort to save the man. He dove again and again, but without effect. Several days later, the Vietnamese dock worker's body washed ashore near Camp Davies.

The soldier explained that no one had seen him whack the man with a piece of board, but several had seen his tenacity, as he tried to save the dock worker's life.

"I caused his death," he said, "and now they're putting me in for a Soldier's Medal. I can't let them give it to me!"

"Just keep your mouth shut and accept it," I told him. "If you don't, they'll have you up on charges."

## ◄◄ Rewind, Cholon, SVN – 15 July 1968

It wasn't just Americans creating bad feeling with the Vietnamese. South Vietnamese in authority created friction too, and a little authority went a long way.

At the Movements Control Center, we had one day a week "stand-down" for haircuts, laundry, and so on. Back in July, my partner, Griffin, was off the day in question, and while alone driving my jeep from the Rice Mill to Cholon, I heard the squealing of brakes and scraping sounds behind me. Looking back over my left shoulder I saw two South Vietnamese soldiers on a white Vespa, a big plastic bag of rice between them, swerving out of control. The rice was first to go. Then, the passenger jumped off as the Vespa's driver brought it to the ground. I slowed my jeep as I looked back. The uniformed ARVN (Army Republic of Vietnam) driver, already on his feet was waving me off, or so I thought. As I pulled away I heard more shouting. The ARVN pulled a .38 pistol, pointing it at me, as he screamed in Vietnamese. He approached my vehicle, sticking the .38 in my face. Three inches from my nose, the .38 looked like the barrel of a cannon. I reached for my M-1 carbine lying next to my camera between the two front seats. I put my right hand on my carbine, lifting it from the bed of the jeep to call his bluff, but the ARVN pulled back the hammer on the .38. *Oh shit, this is it,* I thought, *I'm going to be a spot in history and a dot in time.* I exited the jeep without my carbine, as the ARVN eased the hammer down. He was still pointing the .38 in my direction. I stood next to my jeep, as two GIs in a passing vehicle asked if there was a problem.

"Yeah, there's a problem here," I said, "I think this Vietnamese is going to shoot me. Get out of here. Go up to the Cholon PX and bring back the MPs."

Within minutes, two MP jeeps led by the two soldiers were there, with Vietnamese police – which were known by GIs as "White Mice" because of the white uniforms they wore. As the vehicles approached, the ARVN driver of the Vespa put his .38 back in his belt under his shirt, and motioned for me to get my carbine. I turned around to see the carbine still there, but my camera was gone. The story as I explained it to the police did not seem to make a lot of sense. The ARVN denied everything and was allowed to leave.

About the time I met Ben Barrett, I had also become friends with a lanky, tough, civilian contractor with Philco-Ford. Like all his contemporaries, Mosher, had a brand new Ford pick-up truck and a long-range Motorola radio, which had three times the range of our tactical PRC-25s. When I was not traveling with Ben, Mosher and I ran the roads together. Mosher was my US civilian counterpart, but he made one hundred times the amount of money I did, for doing the same job. The monetary inequities did not keep us from being friends. He kept telling me to get out of the Army and he would get me a job with Philco-Ford in Vietnam.

On a run to Tan Son Nhut the ARVN soldier, who had pulled the .38 on me, waved us through the gate. Mosher smiled and said, "I'll be a son-of-a-bitch. That's the same little bastard who pistol-whipped me, right here!"

He explained that at the main gate several weeks before, the ARVN had questioned Mosher's civilian identification papers. When Mosher would not cower to the ARVN, he pulled his now infamous .38 on Mosher, who ended up spread-eagle on the pavement, with the ARVN's foot on his neck and head. Before the US Air Force Security Police could defuse the situation, the ARVN struck Mosher with his pistol three or four times in the face.

Months later, after I arrived at Cu Chi, Mosher sent word he was paying me a visit. I stood at the main gate knowing the civilian beer and soda trucks would be rolling in at 0900 hours. Mosher's blue pick-up, red light flashing, was not hard to spot.

He was due back in Thu Duc that same morning.

"There's something I had to tell you in person," he said, "no other way to get the communication to you without passing it through someone else."

"Our score with *Marvin the ARVN,* at Tan Son Nhut has been settled. Ten days ago, between Newport and Thu Duc at dusk, I saw an ARVN jeep on the side of the road, its driver was trying to flag down help. I realized it was the ARVN who pulled the .38 on you and pistol-whipped me. It was my turn. I beat the little bastard senseless and threw his ass off a ledge into a rice paddy."

### ◄◄  Rewind,  Gia Dinh, SVN – 10 July 1968

Vengeance wasn't always that sweet or that warranted. As I mentioned, the military vehicle I drove had a white sign below the windshield reading MOVEMENTS CONTROL. To the Vietnamese, we looked like MP jeeps, which read MILITARY POLICE in the same manner.

In July 1968, we were warned, as were the Military Police, to beware of rock throwers.

"Do not stop or chase rock throwers down alleys. Their ploy is to drop grenades in the back of MP jeeps."

But, driving in the Gia Dinh area of Saigon, a Vietnamese civilian threw a rock, hitting my windshield. Adrenaline and anger over took me.  Here I was chasing the rock thrower down the alley, first by jeep, then on foot.  He jumped over a four-foot wall at a construction site, but I stayed on his tail.  A foot deep in water, within ten yards, I caught up with him.  I grabbed him by the shirt and was about to smash him around, when I realized he was only fourteen or fifteen.  I just didn't have it in my heart to hurt the kid.  He wasn't a VC; probably just a dumb kid venting his frustrations on Americans, and what he thought was an MP jeep.  I was not about to create another Viet Cong.  I let him go.

## ◄◄ Rewind,  400 Grant Street, Gary, IN – 3 April 1968

Sitting there at the table with the Wiedemann family, I could not help but think,

*What if the circumstances had been different?  What if their son, hadn't been killed?  They'd still be sitting here at the dining room table, but maybe they'd be reading his most recent letter.  Maybe they'd have received it in the mail today.  Certainly, I wouldn't be sitting here! How could simple changes in little things have prevented Bobby's death?  What if he had been assigned to a bunk in a different billet?  What if he had gotten up to use the latrine, just before the rocket attack?  What if the trajectory of the enemy rocket had been slightly different?  Is what the Army told the Wiedemann family really true?  How is it that some die and some survive?  In some cases, if you don't go looking for it, it's just the luck of the draw.  I thought, It's simply happenstance.*

**Flash-forward ►► Cu Chi, SVN – 14 April 1969**

After Thu Duc, when I got to Cu Chi, the 725th Maintenance Battalion had a five-ton tractor dedicated to our operation at the Trailer Transfer Point (TTP). The tractor driver, who pre-positioned retrograde loads, was a nineteen year old soldier named Cole. He was conscientious, quiet and a hard worker. Cole personified the motto, which was emblazoned on some of our vehicles, *Hold on, We're Coming.* I remember someone once referring to him as, "...the driver with all the muscles, and the face like TV's *Howdy Doody,"* but Cole was no Howdy Doody!

In an operation on 14 April, troops from the 25th Infantry Division killed 198 communist soldiers in a massive enemy attack against a hidden infantry camp, a dozen or so miles northwest of Cu Chi. Thirteen of our 25th Infantry Division soldiers were also killed and three were wounded, but we were oblivious to all this. Like most nights after work, we'd grab a couple of sodas or some cans of beer and head for the outdoor movie with our lawn chairs.

Cole turned his tractor back in at the 725th motor pool and headed, on foot, to join Ben Barrett and I for the nightly movie, *The Killers,* starring Lee Marvin, Clu Gulager, Angie Dickinson and Ronald Reagan.

As Cole parked his vehicle, a US Navy, UH1B Seawolf helicopter flew onto the 25th Medical Battalion's Medevac Pad. Navy chopper pilots were near the scene of battle as darkness fell and heeded the call for Medevac assistance. Exhibiting heroic efforts, the Navy flew into an area previously unknown to them, and brought wounded soldiers to the 25th Medical Battalion.

After off-loading their casualties the chopper pulled off, as Cole walked passed the 25th Medevac pad. In the next instant, the chopper, unfamiliar with the area, hit telephone and electrical wires, and less than forty feet off the ground, dropped towards the roadway. Cole looked up, saw the chopper coming at him and dove for a roadside ditch, as the chopper crashed in flames. Upon impact, the helicopter's main rotor blade snapped off and sheered through the wall of the 25th Med's enlisted club, cutting the jukebox squarely in half. Simultaneously, 20mm rockets were launched from the chopper and blocks away partially destroyed a military police barracks.

The door-gunner on the left side of the chopper, the opposite side from Cole, managed to jump free. As Cole came up out of the ditch he saw the gunner, on his side, with his back in flames, engaged in a futile attempt to release his safety harness. Cole, instinctively without hesitation, went to the man's aid. Cole burnt his hands beating out most of the flames, then unhooked the gunner, rolled him in the dirt, and dragged him into water in the ditch soothing the man's burns. As Cole got the gunner to the ditch .50 caliber machinegun rounds erupted sporadically in all directions.

"We kept our heads down until most of the fireworks were over," Cole told me later.

The first explosions caused by the crash, a quarter-mile or so from the outdoor movie were such a surprise that we all hesitated, not knowing if we should run to the chopper or from it.   By the time we realized that  help might be needed, all we could see was a fully burning chopper and one man, either the pilot or co-pilot, totally in flames running from it in our direction.

As we got closer we saw another man chasing after him in an effort to save his life.  Suddenly, the man in flames just dropped over dead.  This had gotten the second man far enough away from the chopper to avoid what happened next.  The JP4 in the helicopter's fuel tank erupted into a huge fireball, the likes that I had never seen before.  The noise of the explosion was ear splitting as we were all thrown to the ground by the impact.  We learned later, that the survivor, the man trying to save the pilot or co-pilot, was Cole.

The two gunners made it too, but both the pilot and co-pilot died – one of them still in the chopper.  Pieces of the helicopter were found hundreds of yards away from the explosion, while at the point of the crash there was not much more than a big black indent in the ground.

How is it that some died and some survived?  Cole was right there that night.  He did not go looking for it, but he did make a difference.  In the case of Cole it was simply more than happenstance.  I recommended him for the Soldier's Medal. His First Sergeant ran the recommendation round and round in circles and it was still "pending" when I left country.

**PFC Cole kicks back on a truck emblazoned with the motto
"HOLD ON WE'RE COMING"**

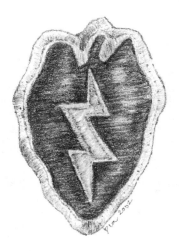

The 25th Infantry Division's "Tropic Lightning" patch was first worn on 25 September 1944, at Schofield Barracks, Hawaii. The representation of a yellow lightning bolt and red taro leaf symbolized lightning fast response and the unit's origin, but was often bastardized in Vietnam as the "Electric Strawberry" by those with no understanding of its military symbolism.

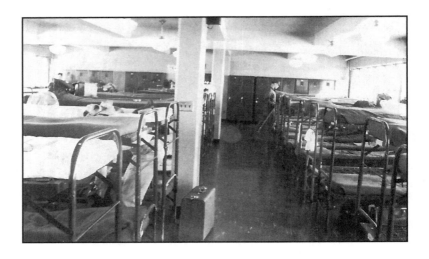

"The paint on the walls had changed from light grey to light yellow, or maybe light yellow to light blue, but the billets at Oakland really hadn't changed since I had been there on my way to Korea."

"I could look out the large windows across the hard-stand, where formations were held, and to the warehouse, where the bodies of soldiers were stored."

## Specialist Fifth Class Robert J. Wiedemann

**"There on a 3" x 5" photograph was the head and shoulders of a young eighteen-year old kid, neither smiling, nor frowning, just looking into the camera."**

(Robert Wiedemann photos courtesy of Mrs. Lillian Wiedemann)

**"Enclosing a photograph of yours truly standing in front of my hooch, with my Thompson Submachinegun."** Robert J. Wiedemann

"The 6 foot python that I traded...for a Timex watch, while monitoring a passing convoy. Our mascot got too close to the snake and 'quick as a whistle' it nearly strangled him."

"The only thing I could relate to was my experience in Korea, when my unit, in combat gear and M-14 Rifles, marched through rice paddies near Camp Mercer." Staff Sergeant Earl Foster, beckons for Private Ray Bows to "move it up" during a Kodak moment.

The shared 25th S & T / Division Support Command movie theatre at Cu Chi Base Camp - to the right the bleachers, to the left the movie screen - behind the movie screen a convenient covered urinal.

Division Support Command area, and beyond the Class I Yard. On the horizon, the perimeter of Cu Chi Base Camp, and to the right, the village of Cu Chi.

Days after the attack of 25 February 1969, Staff Sergeant Bows poses with a captured AK-47.

Just after his arrival in South Vietnam, PFC Robert J. Wiedemann, leans against a 3/4 ton vehicle belonging to the 210th Aviation Battalion, after being initially assigned to the 223d Aviation Battalion, at Qui Nhon.

SP4 Benjamin Barrett on the road between Dian and Cu Chi.

The Trailer Transfer Point at Cu Chi - the hub of operations for convoys headed to Tay Ninh.

South Vietnamese Policeman "White Mice" - Saigon, Vietnam

CWO Paul A. Bows, 1st Cavalry Div while in the Central Highlands, 1965

**The OK Corral - It was from this guard shack that S/Sgt. Bows watched VC through a Starlite Scope, as they milled around in the village of Thu Duc.**

**Major Edwin Rochelle, US Army Transportation Corps, at Thu Duc**

**Captain Mallet, US Army, Transportation Corps, at Thu Duc**

**S/Sgt. Bows, carries the 4th Transportation Command unit flag as a member of the Color Guard at Saigon Port during change of command ceremonies.**

Colonel C. E. McCandless succeeds Colonel DeWitt C. Howell as the CO of the 4th Transportation Command, during the change of command ceremony at Saigon Port, Headquarters Dock, 12 August 1968.

**Joel Mock, while a student at Edison High School, East Gary**

**Joel W. Mock, US Marine Corps**
( photos courtesy of Mrs. Gertrude Mock Miller)

**S/Sgt. Bows presents SP5 Robert J. Wiedemann's flag to his father, Chester Wiedemann, as members of the Wiedemann family look on.**

**S/Sgt. Ray Bows, with his eldest son, Scott, after returning Stateside.**

**S/Sgt. Bows re-enlists at 59th Ordnance Group, Primesans, Germany in 1970, after his return from Vietnam.**

Private First Class Dennis Badore while on duty with the 40th Signal Battalion, Long Binh, SVN, 1966.

Mitsugi Kasai holds a photograph of himself and Dale Buis, taken at the US Army Language School Monterey, California.

Civilian, A. Eversen, on US Embassy courier duty, with a South Vietnamese soldier, Thu Duc, Vietnam, 1965.

Military Policeman, Arnie Eversen while a SP4, on guard duty with the 6/71st Arty, Cam Ranh Bay, 1967.

An avid numismatist and military historian since the early 1960s, combining his two interests, Staff Sergeant Ray A. Bows points out a portion of his collection of military coins, scrip and tokens to manager Charles F. Sowers at the Post Exchange, Fort Sheridan, Illinois after his return from Vietnam in 1969. Bows still collects military scrip and tokens today, including those issued by Sutlers, Post Traders, Post Canteens, Post Exchanges, NCO and Officer's Clubs, and those issued by the Subsistence Department. Bows can always be contacted via e-mail at namlore@hotmail.com.

### ◄◄   Rewind, OK Corral, Thu Duc, SVN – 20 Sept 1968

On 20 September, when I had been transferred from Saigon to the OK Corral at Thu Duc, there were no orders cut. I was just told to go. When I got there, I found the OK Corral was a strange mix. The center of the compound housed the 547th Light Truck Company, to the north, Equipment Incorporated, and to the south, Philco-Ford, which were two civilian trucking companies working on contract to clear pallets of beer and soda from Newport and Saigon Port.

After the 1968 Tet-Offensive, approximately sixty per cent of the Vietnamese civilian drivers working for the two trucking companies never returned to work. They were secretly Viet Cong, and by then, dead on the streets of Saigon and Cholon. Even the "good ones" siphoned and sold gas, pilfered beer or soda from loads or cashed in entire trucks – cargo and all.

The only thing that separated the OK Corral from Philco-Ford was a little walkway, a row of sandbags and a waist high fence. Having potential Viet Cong this close was too close.

I was issued an M-14 upon my arrival at Thu Duc. In addition to my weapons card, I was given a small fifty-cent size brass tag marked number 342, which I relinquished each time I drew my weapon. On the first day, the unit armorer for the 547th said,

"Sarge, you'll have to draw a flak jacket too. What size do you want?"

I looked in over the counter and saw a flak jacket without the collar.  It looked comfortable.  I pointed to it saying,

"What size is that one there?"

"I don't know," he said, "but it's really heavy."

He lifted it off its hook and dropped it on the counter.  I could see it was greener than the normal OD color and lifting it, I realized it was body armor.  This wasn't about being comfortable any more.  It was about having that edge that keeps you alive.

"This one's fine," I said.

"This goes along with it," the armorer said, throwing a big wide belt of the same stuff on the counter.  "It's a stomach protector. You put it on before the vest.  This wider curved part goes down and in front."

Ben Barrett smiled, "Looks like a dick protector, Sarge."

"I'll take it!" I said.

Although, it was only while on convoy from Cu Chi to Tay Ninh that I ever used the lower body armor by sitting on it, which protected me from exploding mines, my armored vest gave me a certain feeling of indestructibility.  I now had a feeling I'd go home with all my body parts intact.

One night, after being issued the body armor, through a Starlight-scope at the main gate, I could see Viet Cong in the village of Thu Duc. The Viet Cong were milling around, walking up and down the road carrying their AK-47s. The village of Thu Duc was not a free fire zone, and all we could do was watch. What were they doing out there? Kidnapping young men and women, forcing them to join their ranks, intimidating or torturing village officials into their way of thinking? Whatever it was, they were up to no good. God, I wanted to pop one...just one!

Within a week we had to preposition vehicles at Saigon Port, and empty Thu Duc of all commercial trucks. An unobstructed view from the south side of the Philco-Ford Compound into the OK Corral could be seen from beyond the perimeter. On the night of the pre-positioning, one soldier, I'll call him Staff Sergeant Winfred, had duties at the far end of the compound in a little two-story building that had just recently been constructed. The "doll-house" for lack of a better description, was painted completely white with a funny little veranda, which served no purpose. Sergeant Winfred was pleased with his duty that night. He had this thing for a big-breasted Vietnamese girl known as Sam. Winfred had volunteered for duty in the "doll-house" to work the night operation with her.

After dark we received sniper fire from the south side of the compound. Several rounds hit the enlisted men's club. One round took out a window at the Philco-Ford Vehicle Operations Center, and several other rounds chewed up dirt in the Philco-Ford parking lot where all the commercial vehicles were normally parked. No one was hit.

As soon as the sniper fired into the compound the lights were cut off. Before we got to the arms room we were bumping into each other in the darkness.

"Don't worry about weapon cards or tags," the armorer said. "Just call out your weapon's number!"

Sergeant Winfred's weapon's number was 338, only four numbers away from mine. I told the armorer that I needed two weapons and furnished the two numbers. I bent down and scooped up ammo already in clips scattered in cans on the porch. I headed for the sandbag revetment, separating the OK Corral from Philco-Ford. As I got there I heard Captain Mallet's voice in the darkness.

"Sergeant Bows, what are you doing with two weapons?"

"Sir, Sergeant Winfred is over at the 'doll-house' with no weapon. I picked up his. I'm taking it to him."

"I don't think that's a good idea," he told me.

"I don't think it is either, Sir."

Before he could tell me otherwise, I was running across the parking lot with Winfred's weapon. I zigzagged across the lot in hopes that the sniper would not zero me in his sights. I heard one unmistakable crack of a Chicom weapon. A few seconds later, I heard another. I had no idea where the rounds hit.

*No sweat,* I thought, *you're not supposed to hear the one that kills you.*

After running a couple hundred yards across the parking lot I slid onto the little veranda at the "doll-house" and lay flat on it. I pounded on the bottom of the door, but there was no answer.

I pounded again.  I wondered if those inside were OK.

"Winfred, let me in," I shouted, "it's Bows."

"Go away, get the hell out of here!" he replied.

"God damn it, let me in, I brought you your weapon."

"No, no, go away, I'm on the floor with Sam."

"Winfred, let me in, you're gonna get my ass shot."

Reluctantly, he opened the door.  I handed him his weapon by flashlight.  I could see by the light that he, Sam and another Vietnamese girl were huddled under desks eating Fritos, drinking soda and listening to Armed Forces Radio, as Van Morrison's *Brown Eyed Girl* played softly from a corner of the room.

"You gonna stay?" he asked,  "I've got you a date!"

"No," I said, motioning for him to unlock the door. "The firing's died down."

I high-tailed it back across the parking lot, without further incident, and returned to where Captain Mallet was waiting.  I had tried to make a difference that night, but my actions were of no significance.

"Is Sergeant Winfred okay?" the Captain asked.

"Yeah, he's fine, Sir…He's just fine."

## ◀◀ Rewind,  400 Grant Street, Gary, IN – 3 April 1968

The second evening at the Wiedemann home, we spoke of many things that had no direct relation to the Vietnam War. I learned that Bobby was a mediocre student. I had been one as well. Wanting to prove himself to his mother, his father and his siblings, he left home at seventeen to join the Army. There was no special girl who saw him off to basic training. I could relate to that. I joined at seventeen myself, and no one special saw me off either.

Even though the kids would be in attendance at the funeral in the morning, they still had homework to do. Joe readied himself for bed, coming back downstairs in his pajamas. After hugging all the family members he hugged me too. Then, Joe trotted upstairs to his room. Mr. Wiedemann and I talked about army life for a while,

"The Army can be pretty tough, I guess," Mr. Wiedemann said. "Dangerous and all?" he added.

I had an image flash in my mind of Private Raymond T. Biglow who had it in for me during basic training at Fort Dix, and how, while on KP, he came at me with a switch-blade. I'll never forget the surprise on his face when I came up out of the *pots-and-pans-sink* with the biggest ladle imaginable and scored a direct hit gashing his forehead. Biglow dropped to his knees. The two big rivets holding the handle to the bowl tore him up pretty bad. His blade disappeared back into his pocket and the ladle went back in the soapy water once the cooks got involved. Everyone played dumb. Biglow had slipped. They took him to the hospital, but later that day he was released and returned to duty.    That afternoon, he came in the mess hall ranting and raving, and pulled his switch-blade, even before he found me back at the *pots-and-pans-sink* in the kitchen.  He tried to stab a cook, and that was it.  The MPs took him away and we never saw him again.

"No, the Army's not really bad, Sir," I replied, "but, some of the people in it can make things difficult."

Then, I remembered that in basic training there was also Private E-2 Haines, the constant kiss-ass National Guardsman, who weaseled his way into barracks orderly duties the night we had force-march during bivouac.  In his absence, I had no choice but to break down his half of the two-man tent we were sharing, and pack his duffel bag.  For the twelve-mile march in addition to my own, I carried his shelter-half, five extra tent pegs and three extra sections of tent pole. The extra weight was a burden, a burden he expected someone else to haul for him.

"Some people aren't cut out for the Army.  They want someone else to pull their weight.  Others just don't care."  I told Mr. Wiedemann.

Then, I thought about Calivere, the card cheat we had at the student company at Fort Eustis, Virginia.  He took me for two months pay in Black Jack.  I didn't figure out what was going on until ten or twelve of us took a train cross-country on our way to Korea.  As we went through a tunnel, just after Ogden, Utah, the light hit Calivere's blue card backs and I realized he had colored in the central diamond design on each ace and face card with blue ink pen.  Publicly exposing him got me nowhere and a couple of his buddies took up for him. He would have been court-martialed if circumstances had been different, if we had been back at Fort Eustis and the First Sergeant or CO had learned of his deceit.

"Others just take advantage of the system, and the soldiers around them," I said.

"I guess," said Mr. Wiedemann, "the Army probably isn't much different from working in the foundry."

"I don't know, Sir," I replied, "I joined the Army right out of high school.  I've never had a civilian job."

### The Funeral, Gary, Indiana – 4 April 1968

The next morning I was up early and donned the uniform that I had prepared for the day of the funeral.  There was no sign that I needed a haircut.  Before I left Fort Leonard Wood, I had gotten a high, tight, close-cropped flat top – *a Double Doble.* The name given to such haircuts because First Sergeant Doble, of the 1st Infantry Division was infamous for telling soldiers,

"Go get a haircut and report back to me, soldier."

When the troop returned for haircut inspection, Doble would bark,

"Now, go get another one!"

Hence, two haircuts equaled a *Double Doble.*  If you did it right the first time, you only needed one.

*Haircut – check!*

*Shoes and brass shined – check!*

*Armband – check!*

*White gloves – check!*

Everything in the lobby of the funeral home was in place as well, the Wiedemann family, the SAO from Fort Sheridan, eight military pallbearers, the NCOIC of the funeral detail, the funeral director and his assistants. The SAO took me to the side reminding me of my briefing at Oakland.

"Most important is that you precede the coffin, beginning now, to the church and to the gravesite. The honor guard will fold the flag and hand it to you. Remember the words when presenting the flag to the family. The flag is to be presented to the father. After you have presented the flag and rendered a final salute, your duties and this detail are over."

We returned to the parlor. Bobby's casket had been turned out straight, enabling eight soldiers, four on either side, to hold it. I took my position in front of it. The detail NCOIC behind me and to my left, said,

"They're ready when you are, Sarge, just step off."

With my first step I could hear the casket being lifted, then, the pallbearers stepped off. We slowly marched out of the parlor. I did a facing movement and with another twelve steps walked down the stairs to the hearse.

I stopped on the far side of the hearse and saluted as the coffin was placed inside the vehicle.  I held my salute until the door was closed, and returned to the survival assistance officer just in case there were any further instructions.

Mr. Wiedemann was standing next to the SAO and said to me, "Sergeant Bows, I want to take Bobby passed the house on Grant Street.  As a child he'd like to drive by the house without stopping, when we'd go from one place to another.  He'd want to ride by and just look at it out of the window.  This is the last time I'll ever be able to take him by the house without stopping."

As we approached 400 Grant Street, I had an image in my mind of a little boy with his hands, face and nose pressed up against the hearse's window, in anticipation of passing his house for the very last time.  He watched the house come in to view, taking it all in, then with an untold degree of sadness, watched it fade away to his right – never to see it again.

As if the image manifesting in my mind wasn't numbing enough, within a mile, what I witnessed on the left side of Grant Street would send me into a stumbling mess for the next couple of hours.  When we passed Bobby's elementary school, the flag was being flown at half-staff in his honor.  Below the flag were classes of second, third and fourth graders, like platoons of little soldiers, their hands over their hearts, standing in silent tribute, as best children that age can stand still in silence.

Did they really understand?

We arrived at a large stone edifice on a corner, somewhere in Gary. It was the Wiedemanns' Church. The hearse stopped at the curb. I helped with the back door as the pallbearers rolled out Bobby's coffin. The back door of the hearse would not stay open on its own, so I held it until the coffin cleared completely. The honor guard mounted the steps with the casket as I stood there. Other people went in the church, and I was still standing there. They shut the doors of the church and I was still at the curb. Bobby's coffin went down the aisle of the church, without me preceding it. I just stood there on the curb. I have no explanation for what happened. I stood there until the SAO came out of the church's side door saying,

"Sergeant Bows, you were supposed to precede the coffin to the front of the altar, what happened?"

"Don't know, Sir," I replied.

"Well, let's try and get the next half of this right, shall we? Come on, I'm taking you in the side door, behind the altar. After the service, you walk in front of the coffin, down the aisle, down the steps, and back to the hearse. Would you, please?"

He felt he had to spell it out for me.

"Yes, Sir," I said.

The next part went well, at least for a while. I followed the SAO's instructions and when the last note of the organ was over, I positioned myself in front of the Honor Guard and the nine of us escorted Bobby's body down the aisle, out of the church, and into the hearse with no further incident. The facing movements went just as smoothly at the gravesite. The ceremony was held in a small rotunda, adequately accommodating those in attendance.

When the eulogy concluded, the firing squad released three volleys and Taps was played with a distant refrain. The eight young soldiers from Fort Sheridan sporting red, white and blue Fifth Army patches had done this numerous times before.

They were sharp and precise. The flag was folded in a perfect triangle with only the blue field and white stars showing. The sergeant in charge of the detail cradled the flag in his arms. He executed pointed facing movements bringing him directly in front of me. I drew my gloved hand up in a slow, deliberate salute. As I slowly dropped my salute, he lifted the flag slightly in the air and rolled it into my waiting arms. He saluted the flag methodically in the same manner as I had just done.

I executed a quarter turn facing movement, and walked three steps to face Mr. Wiedemann standing next to his wife. They were surrounded by other attendees. All eyes were on me, except for Joe. I could see him immediately to my right. I had never seen an eight year old exhibiting a thousand-yard stare before. I have never seen one since.

The words practiced for the last five days were short and to the point.

"This flag is presented in honor of the service of your son,

Specialist 5 Robert J. Wiedemann, by a grateful nation."

I was then to lift the bulk of the folded flag slightly in the air, and slowly turn it in to the arms of Mr. Wiedemann.

But at that moment, as I looked at the family standing in front of me, I remembered the last five days and who the Wiedemanns had become to me; what Bobby's death meant; how great their loss was, and the fact that I could not remain emotionally detached from all that had transpired. I choked and I couldn't get the words out. They just would not come.

"This flag is presented..."

I could not help tears from rolling down my cheeks and the harder I tried to push the words from my throat, the worse it became. My military voice was gone, replaced only by salty, stinging tears and a lump swelling in my gullet. Somehow, the words finally came as I rolled the flag into Mr. Wiedemann's hands. Mrs. Wiedemann touched me on the arm, took a step towards me and hugged me as she said,

"Sergeant Bows, it's okay, it's *really* okay."

Here, was this sweet, wonderful lady who had just lost her eldest son, and she was consoling me. The people at the funeral must have been absolutely stupefied...

Now, as per instructions from the SAO my duties were over, and it was time to go back to Fort Leonard Wood, Missouri and inquire about my paperwork requesting orders for Vietnam.

I guess it took Mr. Wiedemann a couple of minutes to regain his composure, but just after the SAO clapped me on the shoulder and said, "Sergeant Bows, don't worry about it, everything was fine," Mr. Wiedemann again invited me back to the house. This time he insisted I come in civilian clothes.

Within an hour, 400 Grant Street was packed with relatives. Women were walking up the front steps with macaroni salads and casseroles. Food covered the dining room table and people were standing shoulder to shoulder with plates of au d'heurves and finger food. I wasn't inside a minute or so when Mr. Wiedemann reached down into a cooler that had been placed by the front door. He uncapped a bottle of Heineken and handed it to me.

"I believe Heineken was your preference," he said.

"Yes, Sir. Thank you," I acknowledged.

He said, "There's more where this one came from. I understand your flight leaves tomorrow morning. I guess you and I could both use a few beers tonight."

"Yes, Sir," I replied.

"There's too many people in here," he said, "let's go out on the front porch and sit."

Unlike, when I first arrived in Chicago, it was a warm April day in Gary. We sat on the top step of the porch, sipped our beers and watched the cars whiz down Grant Street.

"You know?" said Mr. Wiedemann, "I had often thought that when Bob came back from Vietnam that we'd sit on these steps and have a beer together like this.  When he enlisted he told me, 'Dad, I'm going in the Army as a kid, but I promise you, I'll come home as a man.'  He was happy-go-lucky in grammar school, but by his teen years, he was developing a little bit of a weight problem and some of the other kids made fun of him. He didn't seem to fit in.  Even though he was a good-looking young man, he didn't have a girlfriend that we knew of.  He channeled his energy by going in the Army.  He thought the Army would help him develop into the person he knew he could become.  I showed you his basic training picture.  Now, I want to show you this letter."

> *Dear Dad,*
>
> *I have been with the 1ˢᵗ Cavalry Division, 191ˢᵗ Military Intelligence Detachment for a few months now. Currently, I am at Bong Son, located in the Central Highlands of Vietnam.  We are moving from Bong Son, north, to Khe Sanh where the Marines are having a lot of trouble lately. You may have heard about Khe Sanh in the stateside news.  The story on the siege  up there, is that the operation we are going on could get rough.  My unit will be the first on the ground because we are the intelligence gatherers.*
>
> *Even though I think I was pretty normal as a kid, I guess I caused you a lot of problems and you might say that I had an unhappy childhood.  Just remember none of that was your fault.  Dad, I don't want to worry mom,  but if something does happen to me,  please*

*understand that I am no longer the little kid you knew. I love my job. The people in my unit count on me and I count on them. Just remember, no matter what happens, I am not a little boy anymore, I am a man, and more importantly, I am a soldier, and happy at my job.*

*Your loving son, Bobby*

*P.S. I am enclosing a photograph of yours truly standing in front of my hooch with my Thompson Submachinegun. Hope you recognize me – I don't have much of a round face anymore!*

Mr. Wiedemann handed me the picture that his son had sent him and I stared at it for a long moment.

"Sir," I said, "he's a fine looking young man and a great looking soldier."

The picture I held in my hand is the picture on the cover of this book. I handed the picture back to Mr. Wiedemann. He reached inside the door and passed me another Heineken.

"Sergeant Bows, now that my son is buried, and your official duties are over, I hope you don't mind that I call you Ray?"

"No, Sir, not at all," I said.

"Ray, I had a hard time with this letter. I received it about the same time I learned that Bobby was killed. His 'boy-to-man' transformation was something that I was unable to really grasp, knowing that I would never again see him face to face. But I was able to make a connection when you came to our home. Even though you are a few years older than Bobby, having you here, each evening was a great consolation to all of us. I know there were a few glitches at the funeral, but if everything had gone perfect by military standards it wouldn't have meant the same to us. If you don't mind me saying so, your stumbling attempts to do everything right made Bobby seem a little closer. There were moments, although fleeting, that made us feel that he was back home with us."

I took a slug of my beer. There didn't seem like there was anything else to be said, and besides, I was at a loss for words.

"Ray," Mr. Wiedemann said, "thanks for coming."

Later on that day, I said goodbye to the Wiedemann family.

Never again would I see any of them face to face, but for many years I kept in touch. I consider Chester Wiedemann and his son, Bobby, ultimate heroes to this day.

Twenty-five years after Bobby Wiedemann's funeral, I connected with another family from Gary who lost a loved-one. While researching the camps, compounds and airfields that existed in Vietnam, and the heroic men that they were named for, Joel Mock's story would surface. Joel was from East Gary, a location later renamed Lake Station. Joel was killed one year before Bobby Wiedemann on 21 March 1967.

## Locked Gate, Late Chopper

There is a little playground in a residential neighborhood of Lake Station.   The kids congregate there and play on the swings, the teeter-totter and the children's merry-go-round.

As early as the 1950's, one quiet kid with the last name of Mock, a kid from Warren Street, spent a lot of time at the playground.   When Joel and his friends were a little older they tried their hand at basketball. They got pretty good too. Residents of the neighborhood welcomed the sounds of Joel and friends playing and roughhousing after school and on Saturday mornings.   Even as a teenager, Joel and his friends would find time for basketball back at the playground court.

Joel played baseball, basketball and football throughout high school.  As a  student at Edison High,  he earned· three letters in football and was named Edison's most valuable lineman during his senior year.

Annually, everyone eagerly awaited the "Powder-Puff" basketball game at Edison.  Joel's senior year was no different. It seemed to be that the best and most popular players were expected to dress up as cheerleaders, while the girl cheerleaders would take the floor to defend East Gary's honor against the opposing team.

Joel and his friends were decked out in mini-skirts, hairy legs and all.  Most donned their mother's wigs and in some cases sported died mops direct from Meister's Drug Store.  Under garments not usually found in the boy's locker room were everywhere.  One of the guys was sent out for more toilet  paper to over-stuff big sister's bra.    Joel, however, had a more innovative idea.   On his way to school he had stopped by the local grocery store and picked up two firm perfectly matched grapefruit.  He had thought that he would use them to top off his outfit.   But, at the last minute, he decided against going out on the basketball floor in an over-stuffed training bra.   It was two sizes too small to accommodate the pair of grapefruit, but three of his buddies grabbed him and dragged him out on the floor. He was locked out of the boy's locker room with nowhere to go.

A roar went up in the crowd and Joel knew that the best thing to do was to play along as he had originally intended.   Half way through the first cheer, Joel almost beat himself black and blue with the two grapefruit – but they hung in there, and so did Joel. He kept up with his buddies in jumps and splits and cheers - all to the delight of the crowd.

Then it happened – one of the grapefruit escaped out of the top of the training bra, rolling down the inside front of Joel's sweatshirt and onto the playing floor.   There was a moment of total silence as the left grapefruit careened to half court.   The silence was followed by a roar of laughter.   Joel Mock was the star of the Powder-Puff basketball game that year.

Joel enlisted in the Marine Corps in January 1966.   He was granted leave in July of that year, his last leave before being shipped off to Vietnam.   On his last night at home, a few of his buddies picked up Joel and explained that it was his choice,

"What ever you want to do, Mock.  You're the boss tonight."

"Let's play some basketball," was Joel's reply.    And play basketball they did – until 4.00 a.m.    The last thing that Joel said before leaving that morning was, "There's no place like East Gary."

The young Private First Class arrived in Vietnam in October 1966, the same month that the Dong Ha Logistics Support Area was expanded and the 3d Marine Division moved north towards the DMZ.    Dong Ha, unlike other Marine combat bases was located inland.    The Cua-Viet River was a major supply route to Dong Ha.    Fuel and ammunition were transported up the river to Dong Ha in LCMs, wide, shallow draft, landing craft, operated by the US Navy.    Additional supplies of POL went overland in trucks from ESSO's Lien Chien Terminal near Da Nang to Dong Ha.

Even though the Cua-Viet River was used whenever possible to re-supply Dong Ha, the chancy mission of supplying beyond that point, to Marine outposts further north, was the job of the 9th Motor Transport Battalion, 3d Marine Division (Rein FMF). Joel and a buddy, Corporal Ron Bladt from Atlantic, Iowa were assigned to C Company.

"We shared a tent together," said Ron, "Joel could raise your moral when your day was down.    He was a heck of a swell guy. I took a like'n to him right away.    He was just like family. Besides, when your 4,000 miles from home, Indiana and Iowa are like livin' 'cross the street from each other."

"We used to run convoys to Gio Linh, Cam Lo, Razor Back, Delta 5, Camp Carroll and Khe Sanh.    The first time we went to Khe Sanh, the elephant grass was seven or eight feet high on both sides of the road.  We made a few runs down south to Phu Bai and Hué and on another run to Khe Sanh we thought we were going in the wrong direction 'cause all the elephant grass along the road was gone.  We didn't recognize the place.  We found out that they were using chemicals, although, they didn't have any fancy names for them back then.  A few times we even drank the Vietnamese water along that road when we'd get real dry.  They never explained the dangers of it.  Eventually, they sprayed Agent Orange all the way from Dong Ha to Khe Sanh and just about burned off everything.

"Joel and I would talk a lot.  When we weren't working we'd sit around and shoot the shit.  Sometimes we'd sit and talk about how screwed up some of the things in the Marine Corps were – other times we'd talk about our families.  He got some pictures of his folks once, and I dug out some photos of my mom and dad.  We made a pact that if one of us got killed the other one would go to see his family.

"Most of our convoys were run during the day, but on the 20th of March 1967, the Marine base at Gio Linh was running in short supply of just about everything, including ammo.  Somebody got the bright idea of running the convoy at night; believe it or not they said it'd probably be safer that way.  We did what we were told, no matter if we thought it was smart or not.  About midnight the convoy headed to Gio Linh only six or seven miles from the DMZ.

"I was a little concerned about Joel.  I was his back-up driver and machine gunner.  But our tractor had just come out of Flusey that day.  Flusey is what we called FSLU (Fleet Supply Logistic Unit) Maintenance.  It had been in for a major overhaul and was running fine, but they hadn't gotten the machine gun mounted back on the ring mount. They put me with my M-60 on another truck behind Joel. I kept my eye on him the whole route.

"We got to Gio Linh without a hitch. When we arrived they didn't have the gate open for us. Another Marine Corps screw up I thought. Just as that thought was going through my mind the Army truck, directly in back of Joel, was detonated by a mine in the road. It was carrying 105's and exploded into nothingness – the biggest piece that came back to the ground was a piece of fender shaped like a corkscrew. All Hell broke loose. We were sitting ducks for the Viet Cong who had positioned themselves on the right side of the road. The M54, Five Ton full of ammo that Joel was driving went next. It had a grenade thrown in it about the same time Joel was hit by small arms fire. It was only a hundred yards from the main gate. He managed to get out and off to the right hand side of the road.

"Joel had caught a lot of flak. He was hit bad, real bad. I was kept pretty busy, but I remember that they had a corpsman with him."

Bladt stuck to his gun until ordered into a ditch by an officer because of the heavy small arms fire directed at the convoy. After a few minutes in the ditch, Bladt decided on his own that he would be more useful back up on his truck. He got to his gun and again opened up on the enemy who were completely disconcerted by his actions. Silhouetted against the sky by exploding ammunition on the trucks in front and behind him, he neutralized two enemy positions. Finally, he was again ordered off the gun, but he continued to fire with his M-14 at the enemy.

Then, he climbed into the company wrecker but while he was moving it to safety, heavy enemy automatic weapons fire blew out the tires and disabled the vehicle.

"We called for a Medevac chopper to get Joel out of there. They told us that there wouldn't be any Evac-chopper until we promised them a secure area. We told them we had prepared a secure landing zone to get Joel out, but they still wouldn't come. We fired back and forth most of the night. A helicopter finally came after daylight, but by then it was too late for Joel – he died twenty minutes after they picked him up."

Joel died of "multiple fragmentation wounds, penetrating (the) right thigh, perforating (the) left shin, (the) right buttocks and (the) right side of (the) head." He was pronounced dead at 0740 hours, 21 March 1967. Joel Mock's body was identified by his commander, 1st Lieutenant Nolan, the exec, 2nd Lieutenant Satterfield and First Sergeant Pahnka. The same superiors who called him "a silent Marine who never complained."

For his actions, Ron Bladt received the Bronze Star and was promoted to Corporal for meritorious, courage and initiative.

PFC Joel Mock was posthumously awarded the Vietnamese Military Merit Medal and Vietnamese Cross of Gallantry with Palm. Camp Joel Mock at Dong Ha was dedicated on 27 February 1968. It was erroneously reported that Camp Mock was the third camp in Vietnam named after a Marine killed in action. However, Camp Reasoner, Camp Edwards, Camp J.K. Books and Goodsell Heliport all in Da Nang, and Camp Hill at Gio Linh had been previously named in honor of fallen Marines.

At Lake Station, Joel's football team voted to retire his number. Number 27 resides in the trophy case at Edison High School. The playground three blocks from his house was named in his memory. The kids in the neighborhood still play there – kids that weren't even born when Joel went to Vietnam or when Joel died there. This new generation of children still laugh, shout and roughhouse, and the neighbors still welcome the sounds of them after school, and on Saturdays.

When I last talked to Ron Bladt, he complained of numbness of his right side as well as kidney and lower tract problems. His ability to communicate had also been impaired. His ailments and their possible link to his exposure to Agent Orange, when he and Joel made the Dong Ha to Khe Sanh run, had not been recognized by the Veterans Administration at that time.

"Since my problems started I always act like I've been on a seven day drunk – but I don't drink," said Ron. "Before the problems started I kept my pact with Joel. I went and saw his mom and dad. They picked me up at O'Hare Airport in Chicago, and as soon as I saw them walking across the terminal, I knew they were Joel's family and I imagined how it might have been for him if he had come home safe."

### Final Flash-forward ►► Convoy

Even though much of *my* Vietnam is told within these pages, like Ron Bladt, the flashes still come chaotically and frequently. I have been told that much of what I write is clear, organized and thoughtful and that I give accounts that express the "reality" of my experience, and the experiences of others I write about. So, why do I have all these flashes and memories about Bobby Wiedemann mixed with my own disorganized recollections of Vietnam? Why do they come so fast and furious, and why haven't they relented after so many years?

After Bobby's funeral, I returned to Fort Leonard Wood, and insured that my paperwork volunteering for Vietnam was in place. After experiencing Bobby Wiedemann's death, I felt it was my duty and my obligation as a soldier to serve my country in the combat zone. Even though I had fatalistic thoughts about going, I had volunteered for a deeper reason. I needed to prove to myself that I was worthy to be called a soldier, so I could hold my head up and I could answer questions about Vietnam when asked. Ironically, the questions never came. No one wanted to talk about Vietnam when I returned. Still, my decision to go is one I have never regretted – ever.

I volunteered for Nam with a promise from the Army that if and when I returned, I would be transferred to Europe. File – 13! Some personnel clerk must have thrown my Inter-theatre transfer request in the trash. At the end of my Vietnam tour I was assigned to Fort Sheridan, Illinois, the very same place the SAO, the pallbearers, the honor guard, and the bugler had been sent from to Bobby Wiedemann's funeral. While at Sheridan my greatest dread was receiving orders as an escort, but it never happened. I never pulled funeral escort duty again. I kept in touch with the Wiedemanns for a long time after Bobby's death. I'd send them a Christmas card each year and when I'd see information about veterans survivors benefits I'd drop the information in the mail to them. They had no way of getting such information otherwise.

Even though my duties terminated with the presentation of the flag and the words that I choked on, I maintained contact with Mr. and Mrs. Wiedemann, and received Christmas cards from Bill and Joe up until 1998. I have since lost contact with the family and am still trying to locate them. I was supposed to cut all ties with the family after my duties were over, but I could not make the severance. I couldn't cut the connection.

In Vietnam, I wasn't a grunt or a member of an elite unit. I saw the III Corps area in Vietnam from a "transportation" point of view, much in the same way that Joel Mock and Ron Bladt had seen I Corps, running the roads on convoy. My experiences took me from patrolling Cholon and Saigon, supervising the movement of beer and soda trucks, to running the roads between Thu Duc and Long Binh, and finally running convoys from Cu Chi to Tay Ninh, as NCOIC of the 3d Movements Region, the western corridor which extended from Long Binh, to Cu Chi, to the Cambodian Border.

The guys I worked with, truckers from the 48th Transportation Group, and other soldiers and Marines like them who ran convoys, really earned their pay. Their jobs put their lives on the line as they brought rations, fuel, ammo and supplies to combat units in the most remote locations. Those *Army Transportation types* should have received the Combat Infantryman's Badge. Often, when their convoys were hit, they fought as infantrymen.

The best General Westmoreland could do, to show appreciation for their outstanding service, was to authorize Army truckers the LINE HAUL tab – a small curved piece of cloth, worn on the shoulder above the unit patch. The LINE HAUL tab only came in black and olive drab.  There was no Class-A uniform version of it.  It was authorized for wear <u>only</u> on the combat uniform while in country.

**The LINE HAUL tab authorized for wear *only*
on the combat uniform, while in country.**

My memories of Vietnam seem to be as sharp and clear as they ever were, although, some dates are vague now.  I remember that for two weeks the body of a Viet Cong sat in the intersection of Cu Chi Village propped against a light pole.

"Why doesn't someone get rid of it?" I remember asking.

When they finally did, we were surprised that it was gone.  It had become part of the landscape.

I remember the GI's finger that I found in an Armored Personnel Carrier.  The APC had been hit by a rocket-propelled grenade (RPG), and was headed back to Long Binh on a flat bed trailer. I wrapped up the finger, packed it in ice, and took it back to the unit, then to the battalion and finally to the 12th Evacuation Hospital. Nobody seemed to want it – but, if its owner was still alive, somebody was probably looking for it!

An RPG round could burn through steel like a hot knife through butter. It was pure dumb luck if you survived being hit by one. At a particular bend in the road winding through the Hobo Woods, our convoys were hit seventeen days in a row, sometimes with RPGs, sometimes only by small arms fire. On one convoy in February, taking a new man to Tay Ninh, I was passing military tractors and trailers in my jeep, when the enemy unleashed an RPG. They were aiming at a POL truck loaded with fuel, but luckily they hit an S & P loaded with 40 foot lengths of re-bar - steel reinforcing rods, just as we passed. The half unchained re-bar had spring to it – a lot of spring. My jeep was thrown through the air like a missile launched from a catapult.

I blacked-out when the jeep was hit. Thank the All-Mighty, for the water-buffalo shit and muck piled in the rice paddy that we landed in. And, thank the gun truck company for, *Margarita,* * and the gunners manning her. They put down suppressive fire, while I pulled myself, and my passenger, from under my flipped jeep. We were pretty banged up and both of us had trouble jumping on the running board of a passing vehicle at the end of the convoy.

---

* *Margarita* - One of many "named" gun trucks that accompanied 25th Division convoys in Vietnam. Such gun trucks were generally modified two-and-a-half ton vehicles mounted with 30 caliber machine guns and re-enforced with armor plating. They were the saviors of more than one convoy in Vietnam.

I was cut up from shards of glass.  Most of my body was black and blue and I didn't know I had broken the tip of my left elbow.  When the convoy got to Tay Ninh, I refused medical attention and made it to the *Holy Land,* the airfield and home of the 187th Aviation Company.  I flew back to Cu Chi with the *Crusaders.*  The next day, I hoped to recover my jeep, but I knew it was a long shot.  Was it ever!  It had been stripped clean by the locals.  We left it there, and within the week it was gone.  A friend, Captain Ron Hunter, commo-officer, 2/34th Armor, gave me a replacement jeep that his people had made from parts acquired through the property disposal office.  I put my new jeep in my unit's inventory by simply repainting the bumper numbers.

Days later, I was still picking shards of glass out of my skin.  I was pleased when I noticed my chest, arms and legs were turning from black and blue to yellow.  I had broken the same arm I had worn Bobby Wiedemann's black armband on.  It may be one of the reasons I cannot separate Bobby's funeral from my own Vietnam experiences.  Eight months into my Vietnam tour, my hands were not nearly as innocent as they had been in April 1968, when I had donned lily-white gloves to present Bobby's father the flag.

Some of my experiences are mine alone to keep.  They are things I am not willing to share with anyone, but I am not ashamed of anything I did in Vietnam.  I was not a village rat.  I didn't do drugs or pot and, in Vietnam, I never shot at anyone who didn't shoot at me first, even though, once at Thu Duc, I really wanted to.

Vietnam is a gleaming,  polished  bauble that I periodically take off the shelf and examine. If I don't, it rolls off by itself and gets away from me, sometimes causing a lot of damage. When I look into its shining surface I cannot help but see the face of SP5 Robert J. Wiedemann, who, for me, is the specter and the personification of the Vietnam War.

## ◄◄ Final Vietnam Flashback, SVN -CONUS, 6 June 1969

The commercial airliner taking me home, taxied down the runway for take off. The engines roared and we shot almost straight up into the sky as if we were going into outer space. One guy, in the center of the plane, let out a half cheer as soon as the wheels left the ground. His joy was premature, and GIs close-by him stared him down. Everyone on the airplane was silent during the ascent. We all knew we weren't out of Vietnam yet. When the aircraft finally leveled off and Vietnam was well below us and we were out of range of enemy gunners, we burst into shouts and whistles. The states were still thousands of miles away, so for now we settled back for a long flight across the Pacific.

I thought about my last year spent in Vietnam and felt as though my experience was both the longest and shortest year of my life. I could still hear the crack of an AK-47, and the whistle of incoming, sounds that no Vietnam veteran can forget. I looked around the interior of the airliner. I saw soldiers who had experienced so much more than I had. By the look on their faces, the way they sat in their seats, and the blank stares in their eyes, I could tell that some could not yet believe they were on their way home. I looked around the airplane for Robinson. I saw many black faces, but his wasn't among them. As I asked the stewardess for a refill of my soft drink I couldn't help but feel guilty that there were soldiers still giving their lives in combat, while I was on my way home.

As I sipped my soda on the plane, back in Tay Ninh and Binh Long provinces, four hundred Communists were being killed on eleven battlefields along the Cambodian border. The operation that took their lives began the day I out-processed at the 90th in Long Binh to fly home. Four Americans were killed in that action and twenty-one were wounded. Further to the north, ten US Marines were killed in another action and twenty-four were wounded near Khe Sanh. During my eighteen-hour flight, sixty-five Communist shellings were reported throughout Vietnam. In Da Nang alone, forty-five rockets struck in three separate attacks. Four American airmen were killed and thirty-seven were wounded. Maybe the war was over for me, but not for them. I hoped Ben Barrett, Ron Hunter, Cole, and the other friends I had made in Vietnam, would survive the remainder of their tours.

We refueled in Hawaii, our first chance to get a beer; the air lines didn't serve alcohol on military contract flights. Between Honolulu and Travis, I dozed off. I dreamt I was back in Vietnam, and the dream was as vivid and as real as anything I experienced while there. When I awoke, in a cold sweat, and found myself on an airplane headed home, I wasn't sure what was dream and what was reality.

Then, the same cheers heard over Vietnam repeated themselves when we touched down at Travis Air Force Base, but not one soldier kissed the ground as so many said they would during their year in Nam.

The bus trip to Oakland was outwardly uneventful, yet as the GIs peered out of the bus windows the tension, which was part of Vietnam, seemed to evaporate. There were no bullet-riddled buildings. We were really back in the states. We were safe.

They issued us new uniforms at Oakland Army Terminal. I went to the showers and threw my jungle fatigues in the trash. I hoped that I wouldn't need them for a second tour of duty. This was my first hot shower in a year and I tried to wash away the smell of Vietnam and all the bad memories; but it would take a lot more than one hot shower on both counts.

We were given vouchers for transportation, and we were sent on our way. We were not debriefed – not thanked – simply released. I couldn't help but think about my return to Fort Leonard Wood after Bobby's funeral or the results of shooting the rabid dog back in July 1968 – I didn't really expect "Thank you's" then either, and there were none. Here, at Oakland, it was shades of Camp Davies all over again.

There may have been someone who mentioned "personal behavior back in the United States," but thoughts had already turned to loved-ones at the other end of the flight or bus ride, and no one heard. Some men had only come out of the jungle forty-eight hours ago and seemingly stared blankly at nothing. But, I knew what they were looking at. They were looking inward, at their own souls, and asking themselves profound and important questions that they weren't willing to ask others – questions they would never find answers to. The same questions asked by the first soldiers returning from combat in Vietnam, and those which will still be asked by the last Vietnam veteran.

I jumped in a cab for San Francisco Airport with some other soldiers and eventually boarded my flight home. I looked out the plane's window and saw three coffins going up the baggage belt. Three NCOs on escort duty, saluted as the coffins disappeared in the belly of the aircraft. Now, there was more guilt. Guilt, that lives with me always. Guilt, that veterans must cope with when they return from war and their comrades do not. Three more *Bobby Wiedemanns* were going home to their families in boxes. As the three escorts boarded the plane, in addition to their black armbands and white gloves, I could see their right shoulders were devoid of any combat insignia.

They hadn't been to Vietnam yet. If they had to go, I hoped they would make it home like I did.

**II Pause**

► Play

# Epilogue

## *The Pole-Cat and the Hawk MP*

*This fellow at the bar started talking about the War. Tears of rage welled up in his eyes . . . I pulled up a stool and said, shake the hand of another fool. I was there in 68 and 69.*

These lyrics from *I Ain't Here Alone*, written and sung by our friend, folk singer, and Vietnam veteran, Michael J. Martin have had special meaning to me since hearing them twenty years after my return from Vietnam. I have only run into a few vets since Nam that I knew while there. However, I have met a lot of good men since my return. Vietnam veterans like, Sergeant Major John Holland, Fred Fiedler, Dennis Wood, Paul Samuel, Steve Deliconio, Dennis Drafone, Howard Rollins, Chuck Richards, Myron Williams, Abel Garcia, Stan Martinez, Rick *Two-Feathers* Will, Ted Shpak, Carey J. Spearman, Captain Bob Evans, CW4 Don Joyce, Ed Williams, Dwight Hoskins, Wayne McNett, Mark Hoskins, Ron *Doc* Smith, Ken Glass, Pete Griffin, Mark *Oky* Okazaki, Mike *Machinegun* Kelley, Vic Tejéra, Robert Blackwell, *Sugar Bear* Johnson, Felix of Quai-Docks, Richie Rainville, Fred Danny Fredricks, "Lucky," Lynn Chapman, Lee Dobbs, Andy Shukula, Frank Swygert, Dan C. Thompson, Bob Armstrong, George Bennett, Whit Alvin, Max Wilson, Tom Nolin, Willis, Bob West, Jeff Burstein, Julius Farago, Dana Martin, Charlie Rains, George Williams, Russ Gearhart Sr, Ray McGee, Wolfgang Bast, Charlie Bevelacqua, Johnny McCully, Tony Lackey, Richard Trott Sr, Major John Snodgrass, General Joe Stringham, M/Sgt. Tony Junot, M/Sgt. Howard A. Daniel III, Medal of Honor recipients Sammy L. Davis, John Baca, Gary Wetzel, Michael Fitzmaurice, and Col. Roger Donlon.  I can't forget any of these fine soldiers, including Tim *Doc Holiday* Taylor, and Jimmy *Doc* Perry, who are no longer with us.

Among such men is Dennis Badore who was one of many veterans who attended the launching of my book *Vietnam Military Lore 1959 - 1973, Another Way to Remember* on 15 April 1989.  He got a book, made a couple of wisecracks (the kind he is known for), and went on his way.

He, his wife Doris, and their good friend, Linda Cruchshank, showed up again nine years later in 1998, when *Vietnam Military Lore – Legends, Shadows and Heroes* made its debut.  I autographed his copy, *To Dennis, a Vietnam veteran who did his fair share. Best wishes Ray Bows.*  Linda, who wasn't afraid to say what was on her mind asked, "Is that all you're going to write to him?"

The autograph ended up as, *To Dennis, a Vietnam veteran who did his fair share...and then some!    Best wishes,  Ray Bows.*  The *...and then some!* seemed to do the trick for Linda.

Years went by before I bumped into Dennis again.  I saw him in front of the "Omelet Factory" in Pembroke, Massachusetts, and at first I didn't recognize him.

"I've got some Vietnam reference material you might be able to use," he told me.

We never got together.  I didn't see Dennis again until Washington, DC, Veterans Day, 2000.  It was the same week-end that I met Pia, and we could both see that Dennis' lovely and charming wife, Doris, was the perfect veteran's wife. At our fourth meeting I learned that he supports her in her business, and she supports him when it comes to anything to do with Vietnam. She's a classy lady, and she's always there at Vietnam veteran conventions with Dennis, because she knows how important Vietnam is to him.

Dennis was working for General Dynamics in Quincy, Massachusetts building military hardware when Vietnam broke out. He could have had a deferment, but instead he volunteered to go to Vietnam in 1965. He told me, "It just seemed like the right thing to do." After basic training at Fort Dix, New Jersey, Dennis learned to climb poles at the US Army Signal School at Fort Gordon, Georgia. Then, after fourteen days on the USS *Gaffney*, Dennis' unit, the 40th Signal Battalion, arrived in Vung Tau, March 1966. The battalion was trucked to Long Binh when it was still just a mound of red earth, and pretty much in the middle of nowhere. Dennis' days in and around Long Binh were spent climbing poles, stringing wire for telephones and electrical generators.

Most every Vietnam veteran at one time, or another, saw a lineman like Dennis while in Vietnam. They were the guys thirty or forty feet in the air, strapped to light poles during the Bob Hope Show at Christmas time. Linemen were as at home up on a pole as we were on the ground. Even though they had a better view of Rosey Greer, Ann Margaret and the Gold Diggers for that one special event, there was a big drawback to being a pole lineman. There wasn't a better sniper's target in Vietnam than a signalman at the top of a thirty-five foot pole.

Dennis tells the story of when, five months into his Vietnam tour, thirty-five feet in the air, he heard a familiar voice from the ground shouting,

"Hey, asshole! What the Hell are you doing way up there? Are you sure you know how to climb that thing?"

Dennis' brother, Roger Badore, was recently assigned to the 154th Transportation Battalion at Newport, near Saigon. Dennis never expected his younger brother to show up in Vietnam.

I, like Dennis, had a relative in country; my uncle, CWO Paul Bows, was stationed with the 41st Signal Battalion in Nha Trang on his second of three Vietnam tours. I know from first hand experience that nothing in Vietnam made you feel closer to home than having a relative in-country. Dennis and Roger were only ten or so miles apart and got to spend a lot of time together, mission permitting.

On his last month in Vietnam, Dennis fell from a pole dropping thirty-five feet to the ground.

"I hit the ground with a thud. It took me about a week and a half to recover from the impact, then I went back to work. Poles are just like horses, once you're thrown, you just have to climb back on."

Dennis climbed a dozen poles a day in Vietnam for most of his 365 days there. That's approximately 4,000 poles during his year in-country. By my arithmetic, if those poles had been stacked end to end, he would have attained a height of 120,000 feet, or over twenty-two miles in the air.

After Vietnam, Dennis was transferred to Fort Meade's Headquarters Company 47th Direct Support Group (Provisional) and trained in riot control. His unit was a reaction force if anti-Vietnam War riots broke out in the Washington/Baltimore area. When Dennis was separated from the US Army, he went back to work in Massachusetts, and several years ago he was prematurely retired from his job because of lead inhalation poisoning.

Like the others, Dennis Badore, is not only an example of what a Vietnam veteran can become because he served honorably and faithfully in Vietnam. He goes beyond that. He's a success story because of his beautiful and charming wife, who supports his activities as a Vietnam veteran, and because his service as a Vietnam vet transcends all barriers. When Dennis and I met that third time, we locked in on each other. We both remembered the brotherhood we had in Vietnam, and even though we never knew each other back then, like the other Vietnam vets, I've mentioned, we developed a kinship.

Two years later, Dennis and Doris insisted that Pia and I stay with them when my triple by-pass heart surgery was imminent. Dennis drove Pia from Scituate, Massachusetts, forty-five miles each way to the West Roxbury Veterans Hospital every day, so that she could be with me. He would make the return trip each evening to pick her up. He and Doris gave us a place to stay while I was recovering, even though, fish and houseguests begin to get old after three days.

Dennis' feelings of brotherhood were even stronger than all he and Doris had done. During my recovery we were invited to the home of one of his family members for Thanksgiving.

We stayed at Dennis and Doris' bed and breakfast, the *Ocean-side Inn*, for thirty-one days. They expected us to stay longer.

Many people talk a good game of brotherhood, but Vietnam veteran, Dennis Badore and his wife, Doris, live it. I don't remember when I started calling Dennis, "The Pole-Cat," but it's a name he earned. He and Doris will always have a special place in our hearts.

Dennis Badore, isn't the only Vietnam veteran who has become special to Pia and I. Another, is Arnie Eversen, who served with the US Embassy in Saigon as a civilian, and later returned to Vietnam as a soldier. To my knowledge, there are only a few Vietnam veterans who can wear both medals for Vietnam military and Vietnam civilian service, men who served both as soldiers and in civilian capacities during the War. One of those men was John Paul Vann; the larger than life character in Neil Sheehan's book, *A Bright Shining Lie.* Vann served first as a soldier, then as a civilian. Arnie did it the other way around. He served first as a civilian in the combat zone then as a member of the US Army's Military Police Corps.

 I was a year old when Irwin A. Eversen Jr. was born behind the Iron Curtain, 3 September 1946, while his father and namesake had a diplomatic posting to Prague, Czechoslovakia. Arnie and I traveled in some of the same circles at different times, living in Paris, Brussels and Saigon. Arnie as a State Department dependant and I as a soldier. Arnie never lets me forget that he is younger than I am. On certain occasions he claims that the difference is as much as twenty years, and that his dark hair and beard are due to clean living and the vitamins he takes.

Although there is both that European and Vietnam connection, Arnie and I never crossed paths until, like most of the veterans mentioned in this epilogue, we met at the Vietnam Veterans Memorial. I have met other memorable people at "The Wall," including Bobbie Keith, the AFVN weather girl who I had only seen on TV while in Vietnam. Still a *Bubbling Bundle of Barometric Brilliance,* Bobbie Keith, also shares both a Paris and Saigon connection with Arnie and I. Bobbie Keith still supports veterans and their families and is now a regular National Park Service Volunteer at the Memorial.

A few years after meeting Bobbie, I met Arnie at "The Wall" in 1994. We also locked in on each other, when realizing that we both spoke fluent French. Arnie and I still have a running battle about who's more fluent. *Arnie c'est moi! Mais je vais dire que c'est toi!* His French is actually far better than mine. I wish I could say that Arnie and I were stationed together in Vietnam. He's the kind of guy, like Dennis, that you like to have watching your back. Both are men who still react positively to dangerous or out of order situations.

Arnie has uncompromising opinions about the Vietnam War and, on occasion, we don't always agree. I look forward to our discussions, which usually occur around Memorial Day or Veterans Day or the few other times we get to see each other every year. For many years he has involved himself with the subject of POWs and MIAs and has sat through Senate hearings on the issue. He has also contributed his time to schools in the Washington DC area, sharing his experiences and knowledge with students who wish to know more about the Vietnam War. Arnie is an informed, articulate and methodical instructor. He is an ardent and formidable opponent in debate and, often, I find myself allowing him the last word in our discussions.

Arnie served at the US Embassy in Saigon from August 1965 until August 1966, as a messenger, transporting and safeguarding classified material between the US Embassy and facilities of the South Vietnamese government, foreign missions and US military installations.

For the last six months that Dennis Badore was climbing poles at Long Binh, Arnie was an audacious nineteen-year-old with a cowboy hat and a grease gun running the roads with his Vietnamese bodyguard, or taking classified documents on flights to various embassies in Southeast Asia.

Arnie's story is probably unique in the annals of the Vietnam War.  To my knowledge he was the only American civilian serving in Vietnam in an official State Department capacity to be successfully inducted into the military.  He received his draft notice while working in Saigon, returning to the United States, attending basic training, training in military police techniques and returning to Vietnam as a Military Policeman.  Didn't Uncle Sam realize that he was already doing an important job over there?

After basic training at Fort Bragg and Military Police School at Fort Gordon, Private Eversen returned to Vietnam in February 1967, assigned to Battery B, 6th Battalion, 71st Artillery, which was part of the 97th Artillery Group.  Arnie was assigned to Cam Ranh Bay.  The mission of his Hawk unit was to defend Cam Ranh against attack by enemy aircraft.  I give Arnie a bit of a ribbing about his duties at the Hawk Site.

"Arnie, how many Viet Cong airplanes did your unit actually shoot down during the war?" I asked, knowing full well the Viet Cong had no air force.

"No enemy aircraft ever got past Cam Ranh. We were so good, they were afraid to ever leave the ground."

Beginning in February 1967, Arnie's duties involved, convoy escort and road recon when his battery would change locations. He pulled perimeter defense and manned listening posts, surveying eddies and the potentially unfriendly sandbars that would rise and fall with the ebb and flow around Cam Ranh Bay. At the end of February 1968, as the Tet Offensive was winding down, SP4 Arnie Eversen, was transferred to the east coast to finish out his time in the Army. To this day Arnie's privately owned vehicle sports a license plate that reads "HAWK MP." It's a handle that he's proud of!

Once stateside, he was stationed at a Nike Hercules missile base at Franklin Lakes, New Jersey, as Assistant Section Chief of Base Security. Arnie completed his military service 25 August 1968. Five years later, he was hired by the Federal Reserve Board, where he still works.

Like, Dennis and Doris, and Bobbie Keith, Arnie is always a gracious host. When we visit, he always has a place for us to stay. He sets a great breakfast table, State Department style, and serves the best French croissants in town. Speaking of croissants, one wall of his den is covered with plaques and awards, mostly mementos of his Vietnam service. Among them is a jungle hat framed under glass, the one he wore all through Vietnam, burnt into a croissant shape, or crescent moon, during a 1996 Melborne, Florida Vietnam veterans reunion now known as the "Battle of Wickham Park." You won't get that story from us. Arnie will have to explain his complicity himself.

Arnie Eversen is a familiar face at many Vietnam veteran reunions and every weekday lunch-hour, since its conception, Arnie visits the Vietnam Veterans Memorial. If ever you visit "The Wall" around noon, you are almost sure to see the images of at least four Vietnam veterans there, Frederick Hart's three-soldier statue and our friend, Arnie. We are proud to call Arnie Eversen, Bobbie Keith, Dennis Badore, Doris Crary and the others mentioned in this epilogue, our friends.

Throughout our lives we experience many diverse relationships with the people we encounter, some of which are nothing short of wonderful.

■  **Stop**


⏻  **Power Off**

# Time-Line

A chronological guide to events mentioned in this book.

| From | To | Location and Circumstances |
|------|-----|----------------------------|
| 25 Jan 1963 | 22 Mar 1963 | Bows attends Basic Training, Fort Dix, NJ |
| 21 Apr 1963 | 25 Jun 1963 | Bows attends T.C. School, Fort Eustis, VA |
| 26 Jun 1963 | 29 Jun 1963 | Bows travels on train from Virginia to Oakland |
| 30 Jun 1963 | 1 Jul 1963 | Transient status Oakland Army Terminal, CA |
| 1 Jul 1963 | 14 Jul 1963 | Bows travels on troop ship USS Barrett – San Francisco to Inchon, Korea. |
| 14 Jul 1963 | 14 Jul 1964 | Bows serves in Korea - USA Chemical Depot |
| 12 Sept 1964 | 14 Feb 1967 | Bows serves at RTO Paris, France |
| 1965 - date approximate | | Robert J. Wiedemann enlists in the US Army |
| January 1966 | | Joel W. Mock enlists in the US Marine Corps |
| 15 Feb 1967 | 15 May 1967 | Bows serves with NATO Spt Activity, Brussels |
| 21 Mar 1967 | | PFC Joel W. Mock, KIA at Dong Ha, RVN |
| 18 Jun 1967 | | Bobby Wiedemann departs for Vietnam |
| 1 Jul 1967 | 10 Nov 1967 | Bows serves as advisor to the US Army Reserve, Cheyenne, Wyoming. |
| Nov 1967 | | Bobby Wiedemann requests transfer to 191st Military Intelligence Det, 1st Cav Division |
| 13 Nov 1967 | | Bows arrives at Fort Leonard Wood, MO |
| 23 Mar 1968 | | Bows receives orders for Funeral Escort Duty. |
| 25 Mar 1968 | | SP5 Robert J. Wiedemann is KIA in I Corps near the DMZ, while with 191st MI |

| | |
|---|---|
| 31 Mar 1968 | Bows is briefed at Oakland Army Terminal |
| 1 Apr 1968 | Bows arrives at Chicago O'Hare Airport and is transported, via hearse to Gary, Indiana with Bobby Wiedemann's body. |
| 2 April 1968 | Gary, Indiana – Bows views Bobby Wiedemann's body. That night he meets the Wiedemann family at dinner. |
| 3 Apr 1968 | Funeral Home, Gary, Indiana – Bows attends the wake and again is invited to dinner at the Wiedemann's. |
| 4 Apr 1968 | Bobby's funeral is held, Gary, Indiana |
| 5 Jun 1968 | Senator Robert Kennedy is assassinated |
| 6 Jun 1968 | Bows departs CONUS |
| 8 Jun 1968 | Bows arrives in Bien Hoa, RVN, & spends night at 90th Replacement Bn, Long Binh. |
| 9 Jun 1968 | Bows spends night at 537th PSC, Camp Zinn |
| 10 Jun 1968 | Bows arrives at Le Lai Hotel, Saigon, RVN |
| 12 Aug 1968 | 4th Transportation Cmd. change of command ceremony. |
| 1 Sept 1968 | Bows and 4th Trans. enlisted personnel are transferred to Camp Davies. |
| 15 Sept 1968 | Bows arrives at OK Corral, Thu Duc |
| 15 Feb 1969 | Bows arrives at Cu Chi Base Camp |
| 25 Feb 1969 | NVA attack on Cu Chi Base Camp |
| 16 May 1969 | Bows is awarded the Bronze Star for meritorious service in Vietnam. |
| 6 Jun 1969 | Bows departs Vietnam from Bien Hoa Air Base, arrives at Travis Air Force Base, Oakland, California. |
| 10 Jul 1969 | Bows is assigned to Fort Sheridan, Illinois |

# Associates and Buddies
### Soldiers mentioned in the book in order of their appearance

**Staff Sergeant Robinson** – A really fine NCO I met in Oakland. We processed through the 90$^{th}$ Replacement Battalion and the 537$^{th}$ Personnel Services Company together. Robinson rousted me out of my bunk when the attack at Camp Zinn started. After that night, I never saw him again.

**Captain Kelly Cannon** – the Transportation Officer at Fort Leonard Wood, Missouri while I was stationed there from November 1967 until May 1968. One of the best Transportation Officers I have ever worked for.

**Staff Sergeant Henley** – The NCOIC of Post Transportation at Fort Leonard Wood, Missouri. Mature, responsible and better suited for the position than I was.

**SP4 Ben Barrett** – My best friend in Vietnam. Ben was an all around good guy – quiet, loyal, sincere and fearless. Ben was from West Virginia. I'd give anything to locate him.

**"SP4 Griffin"** – worked with me while in Saigon. For the most part I could count on Griffin. He did something out of character one night and when I left for Thu Duc it seemed we were no longer friends. His name has been changed in this book solely for that reason.

**Captain Ron Hunter** - I first met Ron while on R & R in Japan. He was a friend of my uncle, Paul Bows. We both ended up in Cu Chi and kicked around together although, being officer and enlisted, our friendship was frowned upon. In addition to being a good friend, Ron was a fine officer.

**Major Rochelle** – A tall, lanky officer, who was an old timer for his pay grade. I can't remember now if the major had been enlisted or not. In 1968, Major Rochelle was in his fifties. He was quiet, easy going and I genuinely liked the man.

**SP4 Bryant** – A common enough name that I felt didn't need changing. He was a whining Mama's boy who I had no use for. All Vietnam veterans are my brothers, but that doesn't mean I have to like them all.

**Master Sergeant Wilson** – Again, a pretty common name. No need to change it. He had forgotten the NCO Creed.

**"Mosher"** – For obvious reasons, a fictitious name for the contractor at Philco-Ford. On occasion, Mosher and I hung around together while I was stationed at Thu Duc.

**PFC Cole** – Member of the 725th Maintenance Battalion at Cu Chi. Our Five Ton tractor driver, who saved a Navy helicopter door-gunner's life one night in April 1969. Cole was one of the best!

**"Sergeant Winfred"** – Again, for obvious reasons, not the real name of the NCO I brought the weapon to at the "Doll House" in Thu Duc. Winfred was a good friend and a fine NCO.

**Captain Mallet** – When we were stationed together at Thu Duc and Cu Chi, I didn't appreciate him. Captain Mallet saw something in me that he liked and he requested that I be his NCOIC at Cu Chi, later recommending me for the Bronze Star. Looking back on things, I wish I had given him more loyalty when I worked for him. He is one of the finest officers I have ever served with.

**"Private Raymond T. Biglow"** – I have used his first name, and the first and last letters of his surname. He was arrogant, belligerent and a troublemaker and had a lot to learn. I have often wondered where the confrontations between us would have led, had he not been arrested by the MPs.

**"Private E-2 Haines"** – This name may not even be close, but then again it could be. "Haines" was one of those guys who wasn't worth remembering.

**"Private Calivere"** – Another fictitious name. There is no room in the Army for liars, cheats and thieves.

# The
# Noncommissioned Officer's
# Creed

I am a Noncommissioned Officer, a leader of soldiers. I am a professional and a member of a time honored corps – the backbone of the Army.

I will always conduct myself in a way to bring credit upon the Corps of NCOs, the military service, and my country. No matter the situation, I will never use my grade or position to attain comfort, gratification, profit, or personal safety.

My two basic responsibilities are my mission and the welfare of my soldiers. I strive to remain tactically and technically proficient. Competence is my watch-word. I will fulfill my role as a Noncommissioned Officer. I will provide leadership. I know my soldiers and their needs and will place those needs above my own. I will never leave my soldiers uninformed and will constantly communicate with them. I will be fair and impartial when recommending both reward and punishment.

Officers appointed over me will not have to accomplish my mission. My actions will give them ample time to accomplish their own. I will earn their respect and confidence and the respect of my soldiers. I will be loyal to those with whom I serve; seniors, peers and subordinates. I will exercise initiative and take action in the absence of orders. I will not compromise my integrity, nor my moral courage. I am a Noncommissioned Officer.

# Fiddlers' Green

A poem and reportedly a drinking song written by men of the 7th Cavalry Regiment during the Indian Wars in the western United States, circa 1870.

Halfway down the trail to Hell,
In a shady meadow green,
Are the Souls of all dead troopers camped,
Near a good old-time canteen.
And this eternal resting place
Is known as Fiddlers' Green

Marching past, straight through to Hell,
The Infantry are seen
Accompanied by Engineers,
Artillery and Marines
For none but shades of Cavalrymen
Dismount at Fiddlers' Green

Though some go curving down the trail
To seek a warmer scene.
No trooper ever gets to Hell
'Ere he's emptied his canteen
And so rides back to drink again
With friends at Fiddlers' Green

And so when man and horse go down
Beneath a saber keen,
Or in a roaring charge of fierce melee
You stop a bullet clean,
And the hostiles come to get your scalp,
Just empty your canteen,
And put a bullet to your head
And go to Fiddlers' Green

# Glossary of Military Terms, Sixties Expressions, and Movies seen in Vietnam

**APC** – Armored Personnel Carrier

**ARVN** – Army of the Republic of Vietnam, i.e. an ARVN soldier

**Bien Hoa** – (grid XT 99-12) A city on the banks of the Song Dong Nai River, located approximately 22 kilometers northeast of Saigon. It housed Bien Hoa Air Base and Bien Hoa Base Camp which included Camp Zinn. (See Camp Zinn).

**Buis, Dale, Major, US Army** – killed in Vietnam 8 July 1959. He was in Vietnam only two days when he and Master Sergeant Chester Ovnand were gunned down at Bien Hoa during the showing of the movie, *The Tattered Dress*. In August 2002, I met Mitsugi Kasai who had served with Dale at the US Army Language School at Monterey, California. Mitsugi spoke highly of Dale and stressed that not only was Dale the first name inscribed on the Vietnam Veterans Memorial in Washington D.C, but that he was also one of the finest soldiers that Mitsugi Kasai had ever served with.

**Cam Ranh Bay** – (grid CP055-320) located approximately 180 miles northeast of Saigon. A port peninsula consisting of sand and more sand on the South China Sea. President Lyndon B. Johnson visited the sprawling Army, Navy, Air Force complex during his 1968 visit to Vietnam.

**Camp J. K. Books** – (grid AT 945-800) In Da Nang at Red Beach. Named in honor of Corporal Jay K. Books, USMC CAC Pacification Team, HQ Force Logistics Command, killed in action 16 November 1966, when a 122mm rocket hit the guard tower he was manning.

**Camp Davies** – (grid XS 83-97) Originally known as Tent City Charlie. Located in the Fish Market area of Saigon Port. Named in memory of Captain David M. Davies, night chief of storage, 506th Field Depot, killed in action 2 April 1966, by VC bombing of the Victoria Hotel.

**Camp Mock** - (grid YD 24-59) Home of C Company, 9th Motor Battalion, 3d Marine Division, was named in honor of PFC Joel William Mock, killed in action 21 March 1967. The camp at Dong Ha was dedicated in a memorial service 27 February 1968.

**Camp Zinn** - (grid XT 988-129) At Bien Hoa, it was the first base camp of the 173d Airborne Brigade in Vietnam. Named in honor of West Point Graduate Captain Ronald L. Zinn, who set records in race-walking at Madison Square Garden, and who participated in the 1964 Tokyo Olympics before he was killed in action 7 July 1965. Camp Zinn eventually became home to the 537th Personnel Services Company, part of Saigon Support Command.

**Chicom** - (Ch-eye-com) Chinese communist; applies to weapons and other equipment manufactured in China, i.e. "a Chicom rifle," or "a Chicom truck."

**Chinook** - The CH-47A double-rotor cargo helicopter. Transported cargo, equipment, artillery pieces and up to 33 troops. It was first delivered to Vietnam in 1961. It had a length of 98'3" and a basic weight of 18,500 pounds. In January 1969, there were approximately 300 CH-47s in country.

**Cholon PX** - The main Saigon Post Exchange located in the Chinese section of Cholon.

**Class A uniform** - US Army green dress uniform worn in public and for ceremonies etc.

**CO** - Commanding Officer

**Cu Chi Base Camp** - (XT 65-14) The predominant US base camp for the 25th Infantry Division, located twenty-five miles north-west of Tan Son Nhut at the edge of the Iron Triangle.

**"Doll House - the"** - Bows' nickname for the small supplemental vehicle operations building at Thu Duc which was located in the corner of Philco-Ford's parking lot.

**Dong Nai River Bridge** - (YT 015-055) Route 316 bridge (6 lanes) over Song Dong Nai (river), seven kilometers south of Bien Hoa, one kilometer south of Long Binh, eleven kilometers northeast of Thu Duc, Bien Hoa Province, III Corps.

**"Double Doble"** – A close cropped military haircut, named after 1st Sergeant Doble of the 1st Infantry Division. Soldiers were told to "go get a hair cut and report back to me" by 1st Sergeant Doble. When they'd return he'd tell them, "OK, now go get another one!" Thus, the "Double Doble."

**Equipment Incorporated** – One of two civilian contract truck companies that operated beer and soda trucks from Thu Duc for port clearance of Saigon Port and Newport. Their flatbed vehicles were painted black.

**Flying Tiger 707** – Flying Tiger Airlines, a civilian contractor during the Vietnam War. It maintained a fleet of Boeing 707s and made thousands of flights in and out of Vietnam.

**Fort Leonard Wood, Missouri** – Named, 3 January 1941, for Major General Leonard E. Wood, Army Chief of Staff from 1910-1914. It is located in south central Missouri. In 1968, it housed a US Army basic training center and the US Army Engineer School. The post town is Waynesville.

**Iron Triangle, the** - Viet Cong dominated area north of Saigon designated War Zone D.

**Jigsaw** – A 1968 made for TV movie on the Armed Forces Motion Picture Service circuit, starring Harry Gardino, Bradford Dillman, Hope Lange and Victor Jory. This fast paced yarn is about amnesiac and unwitting main character, Dillman, trying to figure his part in a murder. He teams up with Gardino to find the solution and turns the tables on the real killers. Reviewer Leonard Maltin calls this 1968 cliffhanger "utterly confusing" with "frantic editing." He should have seen it in Vietnam the way we did.

While Vietnam was absolutely confusing with frantic editing, we found this movie to be great. Ben Barrett and I risked our lives traveling through what was enemy territory at night, to see the end of this flick.

**KIA** - killed in action

**Killers, The** – 1964, TV movie, released through the Armed Forces Motion Picture Service in 1969. Lee Marvin, Clu Gulager and Ronald Reagan play ruthless killers. John Cassavetes is murdered by pistols with silencers, among panicking students during class at a home for the blind. Angie Dickinson is dangled out a window until she talks. Lee Marvin dies on Reagan's lawn scattering money, with one of moviedom's greatest lines. The cold-blooded violence was mesmerizing, as if we weren't already exposed to enough. It took us two nights to see this one, after the helicopter crash near the 25th Med.

**Koelper, Donald, Major, US Marine Corps** – An early US Marine Corps advisor 1963-1964. The South Vietnamese Marine Corps unit that major Koelper advised actually stormed the South Vietnamese Presidential Palace in November 1963, during the Diem Coup. On 16 February 1964, while in Saigon, Major Koelper thwarted an attempt to kill dozens of military personnel, when VC sappers bombed the Kinh Do Movie Theater during a showing of *The List of Adrian Messenger*. Major Koelper was killed in the blast. The Koelper BOQ, in downtown Saigon was named in his honor.

**KP** – Kitchen Police – mess hall duties for other than cooks and bakers. Details included dining room orderly, tray man, pots and pans man, outside man, and dishwasher operator among others.

**Le Lai Hotel** – In Saigon, along Duong Le Lai Street, at the corner of Le Lai and Le Van Duyet near the Central Market. The seven-floor enlisted billets for the 4th Trans. Command until September 1968. (See "Old Ironsides").

**"LINE HAUL" tab** – A cloth tab similar to an AIRBORNE tab worn over the 1st Logistical patch (and possibly others), awarded to truckers that ran convoys and who were expected to fight in combat as infantrymen. The Line Haul tab was issued in subdued (olive drab and black), and was author- ized for wear in country only.

**List of Adrian Messenger, The** – 1963 movie, by Universal Pictures starring Kirk Douglas, Tony Curtis, Burt Lancaster, Robert Mitchum and Frank Sinatra.  The five Hollywood superstars are disguised in character roles in this witty thriller directed by Oscar-winner John Houston.  George C. Scott uncovers the identity of a mass murderer who is killing off the potential heirs to a family fortune.  This movie is rated – three stars.  I still pull out my VHS copy and watch it from time to time.

**Long Binh** – (grid YT 046-076) the largest US military post in Vietnam.  At the intersection of Highway QL-1 and QL-15, northeast of the Song Dong Nai River, and twenty kilometers northeast of Saigon.  Sometimes known as LBJ – Long Binh Junction.  It also housed LBJ – Long Binh Jail – the USARV military stockade.  Originally, named Camp Ranger by 2d Brigade, 1st Infantry Division in 1965.

**MACV** – Military Assistance Command, Vietnam.  The senior US military command in Vietnam headquartered at "Pentagon East," Tan Son Nhut.

**M-1 Carbine** – US made Carbine issued to early US Advisors and ARVNs in Vietnam prior to the implementation of the M-16 rifle.

**M-14 Rifle** – The M14, 7.62 rifle was issued to many army units in Vietnam prior to 1966 and to support units right up through the Vietnamesation in 1969, although production had ceased in 1964.

**M-16 Rifle** – The M-16, 5.56mm rifle was the most widely used personal weapon employed in Vietnam.  The Army had 230,000 of these weapons in country by July 1969.

**M-79 Grenade Launcher** – The 40mm short barrel, single shot, grenade launcher gave the infantryman a light compact weapon to cover the area between the longest reach of a hand grenade and the shortest reach of a mortar.  It was developed with a quadrant sight for more efficient accuracy.

**NCOIC** – Non-Commissioned Officer In Charge

**NVA** – North Vietnamese Army

**OK Corral** – (XS 95-94) The 547th Light Truck Company's compound at Thu Duc, along QL-1, approximately six kilometers north of Newport at the northern edge of Saigon.

**"Old Ironsides"** – The nickname given to the 4th Trans. Command's Le Lai Hotel in Saigon, after the 1968 Tet Offensive.

**Ovnand, Chester, M/Sgt. US Army** – killed in Vietnam 8 July 1959. He and Major Dale Buis were gunned down at Bien Hoa during the showing of the movie, *The Tattered Dress.*

**Philco-Ford Corporation** – One of two civilian contract truck companies that operated from Thu Duc for port clearance of Saigon Port and Newport. Their flatbed Ford trucks were painted robin's egg blue.

**Phu Loi Base Camp -** (grid XT 84-18) Along the outskirts of the village of Phu Loi, approximately twenty kilometers north of Saigon. Built in 1965 it housed elements of the 1st Infantry Division and was home to headquarters of the Western Corridor's 3d Movements Region.

**POL** – Petroleum products

**Rage -** 1966, US/Mexican movie starring Glenn Ford and Stella Stevens. A not-so-likeable doctor, Glenn Ford, contracts rabies and races against the clock across the desert to get medical help. Movie critic Leonard Maltin calls the film "overstated drama," but obviously I was really taken with it!

**R & R** – abbreviation for "Rest and Recuperation" – furlough taken during a soldier's one year tour in Vietnam. One week *out-of-country* R & R could be Australia, Bangkok, Hawaii, Hong Kong, Kuala Lumpur, Penang, Singapore, Taipei or Tokyo. Three day *in-country* R & R was either China Beach - Da Nang, Nha Trang or Vung Tau.

**RPG** – Communist "Rocket Propelled Grenade"

**Rice Mill** – (XS 808-875) A compound located in a tributary of the Saigon River at the southern edges of Cholon. Home to the 79th Ordnance Battalion (later redesignated the 79th Maintenance Battalion). The compound consisted of buildings once part of a rice mill storage facility.

**Saucer Cap** - US Army Class-A green uniform headgear with black leather visor and round flat top. It was worn with either enlisted insignia or officer eagle and gold braid affixed.

**SAO** – Survival Assistance Officer

**Shake 'n' bake** – A young sergeant who earns his rank quickly through NCO schools, or accredited learning with little overall time in service.

**"Shit-box"** – The way it is used in this book indicates an old junk of a vehicle with a certain amount of resentment attached to the fact that the US Army didn't have enough military jeeps to go around for us to perform our mission at Movements Control Center.

**SOP** – Standard Operating Procedure

**S & P** – "Stake and Platform" trailer - the military term for the flat bed trailer of an eighteen-wheeler. Pia, now you know!

**Tattered Dress, The** – 1957, CinemaScope movie starring Jean Crane and Jeff Chandler. Story of a lawyer played by Chandler defending a society couple accused of murder. Jean Crane plays Chandler's sympathetic wife. When Dale Buis and Chester Ovnand were gunned down in 1959, it was reported in the press that "two Americans were killed by Viet Cong as they watched *The Tattered Dress* starring Jean Crane." Which read better "than …as they watched *The Tattered Dress* starring Jeff Chandler!"

**Tay Ninh** – (grid XT24-47) A city approx. 100 kilometers west-northwest of Saigon, near the Cambodian Border. It was ten kilometers south of the Black Virgin Mountain (Nui Ba Dinh). The base camp (grid 143-518) was located three kilometers west-southwest of the city. The road from Cu Chi to Tay Ninh through the Iron Triangle was traveled only by escorted convoy.

**TDY** – Temporary Duty

**Tet-Offensive 1968** - on 30 January 1968, at dawn, on the first day of the Tet (Lunar New Year) truce, Viet Cong forces supported by large numbers of NVA troops, launched the largest and best coordinated enemy offensive of the Vietnam War, driving into the center of South Vietnam's seven largest cities, and attacking thirty provincial capitals from the Mekong Delta to the DMZ. By the end of that week, the Viet Cong suffered complete military defeat. Militarily, Tet was a US victory, but psychologically and politically, because of the way it was reported in the press, it was a US disaster.

**Valley of the Dolls** – 1967, Panavision movie with Barbara Parkins, Patty Duke, Susan Hayward and Sharon Tate. Adaptation of Jacqueline Susann's novel about three young women in show business. In Leonard Maltin's 2003 *Movie and Video Guide* this movie is rated as a "Bomb." It probably was - I don't remember. I was watching this movie while back at the funeral home the funeral director surreptitiously opened Bobby Wiedemann's coffin.

**VC** – abbreviation for Viet Cong

**1ˢᵗ Cavalry Division** – The major Airmobile Division in Vietnam. It arrived 11 September 1965 and departed Vietnam 29 April 1971. Originally based at An Khe, it spent time in I Corps and Phuoc Vinh in III Corps. SP5 Robert J. Wiedemann was assigned to this division at the time of his death.

**3d Movements Region** – Designated by III Corps – The area of transport responsibility of the 3d Transportation Center, (originally the Movements Control Center under the 4ᵗʰ Trans. Command) which briefly became a USARV unit, but after only a few weeks fell under the 1ˢᵗ Logistical Command.

**4ᵗʰ Transportation Command** – arrived in Vietnam 8 August 1965 from Fort Eustis, Virginia. Controlled most transportation functions until diminished in early 1966. Then its operation was centered around Saigon Port. Enlisted of the 4ᵗʰ were billeted at the Le Lai Hotel until September 1968, when they moved to Camp Davies. The unit departed Vietnam, 26 June 1972.

**7.62 round** – numerical designation of the cartridge for the M-14 rifle.

**11ᵗʰ Armored Cavalry Regiment** – This unit known as the Black Horse arrived in Vietnam 8 September 1966, and departed 5 March 1971. During the author's time in Vietnam, it was headquartered at Xuan Loc and Long Giao and operated throughout the III Corps area.

**25<sup>th</sup> Infantry Division** – The Tropic Lightning Division, was deployed from Schofield Barracks, Hawaii, arriving in Vietnam beginning 28 March 1966. It departed Vietnam 8 December 1970. The headquarters of the 25<sup>th</sup> was based in Cu Chi where it remained during its time in Vietnam. Ray Bows was attached to the 25<sup>th</sup> from February to June 1969.

**40th Signal Battalion** - arrived in Vietnam 21 August 1966. Located at Long Binh until their departure on 28 June 1972, they initially served with the 1st Signal Brigade. On 22 August 1966, they were placed under the 2d Signal Group, and under the 160th Signal Group on 28 August 1967. They were responsible for the installation of fixed-plant communications cable in Vietnam, and also performed rehabilitation of existing indigenous lead-covered cable, field cable, open wire circuits and other field cable tasks.

**41st Signal Battalion** - arrived in Vietnam 24 July 1965, located at Qui Nhon under the 2d Signal Group. In charge of communications in I Corps and II Corps, and later being limited to responsibility for II Corps coastal area, providing communications center, switchboard, radio and multi-channel communications facilities. In 1966, they transferred to the 21st Signal Group, and then under the 1st Signal Brigade from December 1971. They left Vietnam on 27 February 1972.

**48<sup>th</sup> Transportation Group** – carried out motor transport operations in the III and IV Corps Tactical Zones, including line haul and convoy operations. It arrived in Vietnam 8 May 1966 and was inactivated August 1970.

**71st Artillery (HAWK Missile)** - Motto: UNDIQUE VENIMUS, The 6th Battalion, 71st Artillery, a mobile HAWK missile battalion, arrived in Vietnam on 29 September 1965, and was located at Qui Nhon. The battalion was relocated to Cam Ranh Bay, as part of the 97th Artillery Group in 1966. It remained there until it departed Vietnam on 22 September 1968.

**90<sup>th</sup> Replacement Battalion** – The 90<sup>th</sup> Replacement Battalion received, controlled, oriented, billeted, messed and processed in-country replacements for onward movement, as well as personal scheduled to return to the United States. It was located under USARV at Long Binh from 30 August 1965 until 29 March 1973. In 1968 it had strength of 53 permanent party.

**191st Military Intelligence Detachment** – came to Vietnam from Fort Benning, Georgia on 15 September 1965. Its military intelligence functions were in direct support of the 1st Cavalry Division. It was stationed at An Khe, Camp Books, Camp Evans and Phouc Vinh during the war. It departed Vietnam, 15 August 1972.

**223d Aviation Battalion** - arrived in Vietnam on 15 May 1966 and stationed at Qui Nhon. They were activated as part of the 17th Aviation Group and provided aviaiton support in II Corps. They moved to Dong Ha in March 1971 and in July they became part of the 11th Aviation Group. They left Vietnam on 1 April 1972.

**242d Aviation Company (Muleskinners)** – Came to Vietnam from Fort Benning, Georgia on 12 August 1967. Its aviation functions were in direct support of the 25th Infantry Division. It was stationed at Cu Chi until it departed Vietnam 1 October 1971. On 26 February 1969, it lost 9 helicopters on the ground at Cu Chi Base Camp.

**554th Engineer Battalion** – performed heavy construction tasks including construction of bases, structures, roads, airfields, bridges and pipelines. It arrived in Cu Chi, 14 April 1967 and was assigned to the 79th Engineer Group for most of its service in Vietnam. The unit departed 1 March 1972.

**716th Military Police Battalion** – Arrived in Vietnam 24 March 1965. It enforced military law, orders and regulations, controlled traffic, handled prisoners of war, and operated check points and route security. It departed Vietnam 29 March 1973. It served at Tan Son Nhut during its time in Vietnam.

**720th Military Police Battalion** - arrived in Vietnam 19 October 1966. It enforced military law, orders and regulations, controlled traffic, handled prisoners of war, and operated check points and route security. It departed Vietnam 13 August 1972. It served at Long Binh during most of its time in Vietnam.

# Bibliography

**The Vietnam War, An Almanac**
by World Almanac Publications, 1985, Bison Books Corporation

**US Army Uniforms of the Vietnam War**
by Shelby Stanton, 1989, Stackpole Books

**Vietnam Order of Battle**
by Shelby Stanton, 1981, US News and World Report

**Where We Were in Vietnam** by Michael P. Kelley, 2002, Hellgate Press

**2003 Movie and Video Guide**
by Leonard Maltin, 2002, Penguin Books

*Information about Dale Buis, Chester Ovnand & Don Koelper*
**Vietnam Military Lore 1959-1975, Another Way to Remember**
by Master Sergeant Ray Bows, 1988, Bows & Sons Publishing

**Vietnam Military Lore - Legends, Shadows and Heroes,**
by Master Sergeant Ray Bows, 1997, Bows & Sons Publishing

*Locked Gate, Late Chopper (Joel Mock's Story)*
Letters and telephone interviews with Joel Mock's mother, Mrs. Gertrude Miller, and Ron Bladt. Material prepared for **The Vietnam Chronicles - Hearts of Valor** to be published at a future date.

**Army Transportation Association Vietnam** (ATAV), www.atav.us
307, Adair Street H6, Decatur, Georgia 30030.

**1/5th Bobcats Website**, (http://www.bobcat.ws/history1968.html)

**"Johnny Comes Marchin' Home" CD** by Michael J Martin & Tim *Doc Holiday*
1986, MJMmusic.com.

**"Just Push Play" CD** by Aerosmith,
2001, Sony Music Entertainment Inc.

# Acknowledgements

Our sincere thanks to the Wiedemann family.
To Mr. Chester and Mrs. Lillian Wiedemann,
To Bill, and his sisters, Marilyn and Betsy, and their younger brother, Joe

Marie Ambre, Peter Dombrowski and John Ambre

Mrs. Gertrude Miller, Mother of Joel Mock
Ron Bladt, comrade in arms of Joel Mock

Tom Clark, History Department,
Lake Central High School, St. John, Indiana

CWO Paul A. Bows, US Army, Retired
Our mentor – for his comments, suggestions and technical expertise

Our sincere gratitude to Dennis Badore and Doris Crary

General Joseph Stringham, US Army, Retired and his lovely wife, Sandy

Our brother and comrade, Arnie Eversen

Bobbie Keith, the former AFVN Weather Girl, for her constructive criticism,
friendship, and intimate knowledge of South Vietnam, *Thank you, Bobbie*

Noonie Fortin, 1SG, USAR , Retired, M/Sgt Howard Daniel, III, US Army, Retired
and Michael Kelley, for their reviews, suggestions and comments in the final stages

Jenny Ori, for her friendship, inspirations and hospitality. *Merci Beaucoup, Jenny*

Sean Booker of International RV Park and Campground,
Daytona Beach, Florida - *Thank you, Sean*

Major John Snodgrass, US Army, Retired, 1/5th Mech, 25th Infantry Division,
for his interest, and for keeping me honest in all things regarding the 25th.

Carol Morrow, for her suggestions and initial editing of the original manuscript.

Fellow veteran, Oscar S. Mayers, Sr. "Sarge" who is always a gracious host

Sean Eversen, for French translations

Our friend, Ted Shpak, for being so good to us - *thanks for your support, Ted*

Joseph Nemeth and Scot McCoy at Office Depot, Ormond Beach, Florida

Joanne E. Jones, Librarian
Massasoit Community College, Brockton, Massachusetts

The staff at Ormond Beach Library, Ormond Beach, Florida

Al Furtado, Member of Army Transportation Association Vietnam, the ATAV,
(http://134.198.33.115/atav/4tctasks.htm), *Thank-you, Al*

Gina Queleroso Problemi, for being the best Mum in the world
*Grazie, per tutto che fai e hai fatto per noi*

Maria Di Trolio for her encouragement and advise on formatting

Lucia Problemi for always being there, for her expertise in many areas including
formatting, and for her constructive comments - *Thank you, Lucia*

The Oliffes - Franca, Tina, and Gemma for their encouragement

Michela Di Trolio, for her adventurous spirit and her ability to send us on near
impossible quests which we succeed at, and to her brother, Joe Di Trolio

Flavia Coccia Di Domenico, for her lifelong friendship, and for always believing

Andy, Emilio, Mike *DiDi*, Michele, Colin and Aldo

John A. MacPhelemy, Sr. and his son, John A. MacPhelemy, Jr.

Donald L. Bows and his wife, Pat, for all their help

Scott Bows, K. Jeff Bows, Steve and Salle Bows, for their ground breaking work
with all that has come before when projects on Vietnam were in their infancy

Mark Bows for his encouragement, enthusiasm
and for coordinating certain aspects in the production of this book

Joe Delgado, Chief of Voluntary Services,
Veterans Administration Headquarters, Washington D.C.

General Creighton Abrams Jr. of the Army Historical Foundation

General Harold Moore, US Army, Retired, and Joe Galloway,
authors of, *We Were Soldiers Once...And Young*

Mitsugi Kasai, US Army, Retired, Regional Coordinator,
Japanese American – Korean War Veterans

Michael J. Martin, and the Vietnam veterans mentioned in the Epilogue

Carolyn Zsoldos, our favorite Desert Storm veteran

Ben Barrett and my Vietnam associates and buddies

Our good friend, Cuong Le, and his lovely family

Mr. & Mrs. Thoi, Mike Thoi, Thai, Duong, Sonny, Tan Kim Chau,
Tan Kim Thai and friends at the Nam-Viet Restaurant, Arlington, Virginia

Daniel Arant for his professional photography and his sustained research support

Laraine Hinson Spearman, Ann Herd, and Pattie "Blue" Hanlon

Ed Williams, Steve Barrett, and Tim Kelly

Jay McBride and Lance Wilson

Doctor Sammy Nawas, Doctor Vladimir Birjiniuk, Doctor Henri Tannas,
and the staff at the West Roxbury Veterans Medical Center in Boston, Mass.

Kathi Carlson, ARNP

Marilyn MacQuarrie, LCSW, Daytona VA Outpatient Clinic, Florida

Doctor Alan Goldsmith, Doctor Eleanor B. Sorressa, and the staff at
Ormond Memorial Hospital, Florida, including Scott Kelley, Greg,
Arlene, Candy, Hope, Mildred, Rita, Sharlar, and the staff at the
ER, Oceanside Hospital, Ormond Beach, Florida

and to, Cheryl Haab of Sheridan Books for her patience, tenacity and perseverance

# Index

**Miss Pia Problemi** is a British citizen whose interest in the Vietnam War has taken her on an insightful journey. In May 1995, she picked up her first Vietnam book, a *student coursework* book, while working at Hendon School in London. After reading every book available on Vietnam, she traveled to Southeast Asia in 1998. From My Tho to Dien Bien Phu, she met the Vietnamese people and captured their lives with her sketches and pencil drawings. In January of 2000, she learned of the Vietnam Veterans Memorial in Washington, DC and set out on her second quest to learn more about the after-effects of the Vietnam War. On 9 November 2000, she encountered author, Ray Bows, at which time they began collaboration on several projects relating to the War in Vietnam, and Vietnam veterans.

**Master Sergeant Ray Bows, US Army (ret.)** spent twenty years on active duty with the United States Army, sixteen overseas. He served in Vietnam from June 1968 to June 1969. He is a recipient of the Bronze Star, the Meritorious Service Medal, and the Joint Service Commendation Medal among other awards. Bows is an expert on the military tokens and currency of the Vietnam War. He has written for the European edition of the *Stars and Stripes, Military Magazine, BRAVO Veterans Outlook, The Token and Medal Society Journal, NTCA's Talkin Tokens, World Coin News,* and is the author of four books on Vietnam. His poem, *The Tiger That Ate The Fire Base*, written in 1998, was inspired by an actual event. Residing in Edgewater, Florida, he travels with Pia, throughout the United States for veteran related issues.

159